Affinity Publisher 2.0 For Book Formatting

AFFINITY PUBLISHER 2.0 FOR SELF-PUBLISHING - BOOKS 1 AND 2

M.L. HUMPHREY

CONTENTS

Affinity Publisher 2.0 For Book Formatting Part 1

CONTENTS

CONTENTS (CONT.)

INTRODUCTION

This book is meant to teach you how to use Affinity Publisher 2.0 to format the interior of a basic print title that uses a small accent image. We will walk through from start to finish how to create your master pages, how to build your document, how to add text, how to format that text, etc. all the way through to how to generate the finished PDF for upload to KDP Print, IngramSpark, or any other printer you may want to use.

Before we begin, though, it is important that you know which version of Affinity you are using, because some of the options we're going to discuss here, such as studios and panels, were moved around in Affinity Publisher 2.0 compared to the original Affinity Publisher.

HOW TO TELL YOUR AFFINITY VERSION

I am working on a Windows computer and there Affinity Publisher 2.0 is shown as Affinity Publisher 2, whereas the original program shows as just Affinity Publisher, as you can see here:

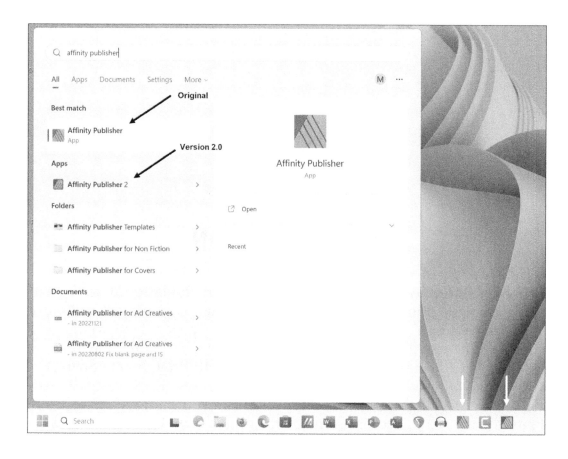

They also have slightly different thumbnails. If you look at the bottom right of the screenshot, you can see how the thumbnail for 2.0 (on the right) has a darker appearance to it and a stronger border around the edge.

You'll also be able to tell which version of Affinity you're working in when you open the program because they changed the appearance of the icons.

Here is the left-hand side of the main workspace of both the original Affinity Publisher (which I've labeled 1.0 on the left) and Affinity Publisher 2.0 (on the right):

For example, one of the tools we will use is the Frame Text Tool which is that icon at the top of the left column that has a T in it. You can see that in the original Affinity Publisher the T used for the icon was written in a serifed font, but the Affinity Publisher 2.0 version uses a non-serifed font.

IS THIS THE RIGHT BOOK FOR YOU?

This book will walk you through how to use Affinity Publisher 2.0. If you have 1.0 instead, which is possible if you bought Publisher prior to late 2022, then the book you want is *Affinity Publisher for Fiction Layouts*.

You could still use this book, but keep in mind that things may be in different locations or look a little different. Concepts will be the same regardless, how and where will not.

If you are trying to translate between this book and the original version of Affinity Publisher, it may help to check out the videos I've posted on my YouTube channel which walk through various tasks in Affinity that are referenced here.

MY QUALIFICATIONS

Okay. Getting back to using Affinity Publisher for print layouts.

My background is in self-publishing, meaning that I write and then format and publish my own books. At this point between hard cover, regular print, large print editions, and collections, I've published well over two hundred print titles both in fiction and non-fiction. Some of my non-fiction is very image-heavy. For example, I have a few books with almost 200 images in them.

When I first started, I did all of this using Microsoft Word, which is a viable option. My most popular book to-date is still formatted in Word. (Breaks and styles are the key if you're going to use Word, but image resolution can be an issue.)

Later I used tools like Vellum, which really streamlined the process, especially for fiction titles. With Vellum you can take an ebook you've created in that program and have a print book with the click of a button. Other options out there include Draft2Digital's platform and I also believe Atticus although my experience with those is limited.

But for me I needed more control, especially on the non-fiction side. That's how I found my way to Affinity Publisher, which is similar to Adobe InDesign but doesn't require a subscription fee. (At least as of now it is still a one-time purchase.)

At this point I have formatted probably over a hundred titles in Affinity Publisher and am very pleased with it. I will note here that most of those were done in the original Affinity Publisher so I am writing this book from the perspective of "I know how to do it in the original version, where is it in 2.0?"

Now, to be clear: I do not have a professional publication background, so it is possible I will use different terminology than the pros or that I may do things in my own, weird, quirky way that works for me but isn't the "best" way to do it. My approach to learning things is to dive in and get it working well enough that I can get on to the next thing, so I am not promising you that I know every single way to do everything in Affinity Publisher. I'm just promising you that this way works, isn't time consuming, and will give you a nice finished product.

HOW THIS IS GOING TO WORK

The rest of this book is going to walk you through how to create a basic print title from start to finish, including how to set up master pages, flow your text, and create and apply text styles. We'll also cover how to export your final product. The print title we're going to create will use a small accent image so that you can see how to incorporate that with your text.

I'll then show you a few tricks so that you don't have to do this level of work ever again. (Once you have your first print layout created, it's pretty easy to use it again and more than halve the required time to create your next title.)

ADDITIONAL RESOURCES

Affinity has excellent help resources. I highly recommend looking at the videos available on their website under the Learn tab up top if you ever get stuck. Here is the link for Publisher on Desktop: https://affinity.serif.com/en-us/learn/publisher/desktop/

(This is how I initially learned the program, but for me the videos weren't in an intuitive order, so I only realized that they covered everything I needed about two thirds of the way through watching them. Hence the reason I wrote the first version of this book.)

They also have an excellent support community and user forums. I usually find relevant discussions via a web search for Affinity Publisher and whatever it is I need to know more about. So, "Affinity Publisher flow text", for example.

Keep in mind, though, that they are updating the product on a regular basis and that 1.0 versus 2.0 are different, so if you find an old answer it may no longer be applicable. Something that you couldn't do before may now be possible or where an option is located may have changed.

They do also have an Affinity Help website that you can access in the top menu of Affinity Publisher under Help or by searching on the internet for Affinity Publisher Help. It's best to access it through the program to make sure you access the version that corresponds to Affinity 2.0.

You can search there as well, although for me personally that is usually my last stop. You need to know the proper terms to find what you want and then sometimes the explanations assume a graphic design level of knowledge that I, at least, don't have.

ASSUMPTIONS

I am going to assume some basic knowledge of how programs like this one would work. Meaning I'm not going to define for you here terms like dialogue box, dropdown menu, control shortcut (Ctrl + C), etc. I do define those terms in my beginner Word books and they may actually be visible in preview if you need that. And you'll have screenshots here, too. But if you aren't at least that familiar with working in software programs, this may be a big stretch for you.

You should be comfortable working in a word processing program like Word before you try to tackle Affinity Publisher. (In my opinion. Try if you want, but it will be harder for you.)

I'm also going to assume that you have basic familiarity with how print books are formatted. I may define things like front matter, back matter, or discuss where to start chapters in passing, but it is not going to be the focus of this book.

Okay, then. Let's get started and open Affinity Publisher.

GETTING STARTED

I'm going to assume that you've already purchased and downloaded Affinity Publisher. If not, you can do that at https://affinity.serif.com/en-us/ or the equivalent site in your country. (I believe that en-us is the part that says United States and in English.)

Go ahead and open it now. The version I'm working in is 2.0.4. This is what it looks like for me when I open it:

It has a New dialogue box visible in the center of the screen with the main workspace visible behind that, although they are the same color so do blend a bit.

To work on a project in Affinity Publisher you need to create a document. You can either choose one using the New dialogue box or, if that's closed, use the File menu up top, which is usually what I use to reopen a recent file.

But for now we don't need to create a document because I want to set up your workspace first. So click on the X in the top right corner of the New dialogue box to close it. You should now see the default workspace that Affinity gives you:

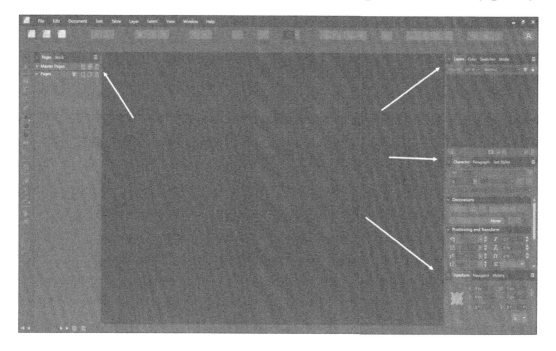

On both sides of the workspace there are panels docked by default. These are essentially task panes that give you options related to specific functions you might want to perform.

For example, the Pages panel, in the top left, shows your master pages as well as any pages that you've added to create your document. The Layers panel, in the top right, shows the layers on a given page—all of your images or text frames in our case.

The panels you see by default in Affinity Publisher are just a dozen or so of the panels that are actually available to you. If you want to see all of the available panels, go to the Window option at the top of the screen. Most of the dropdown menu you'll see below that are panels that you can choose to display in your workspace.

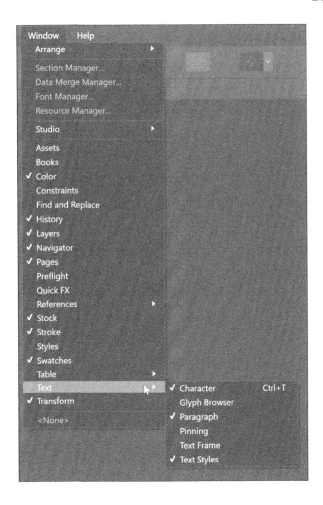

The list starts with Assets and goes down to Transform. References, Table, and Text all have secondary dropdown menus that show more panel choices. In the screenshot above you can see the Text secondary dropdown menu.

(Note that this is different from the original Affinity Publisher where they were under View in the top menu and the panels were all listed under a Studio secondary menu.)

If a panel is already visible, it shows a white check mark to the left of the name. You can see that with Color, History, and Layers, for example.

To close a panel that's open that you don't want, click on its name in the dropdown.

You can also close a panel from the main workspace by left-clicking and dragging the panel from its name tab so that the panel is no longer docked. Once you have it isolated, click on the X in the top right corner of the panel.

Here I have left-clicked and dragged the Stock panel so that it is standalone:

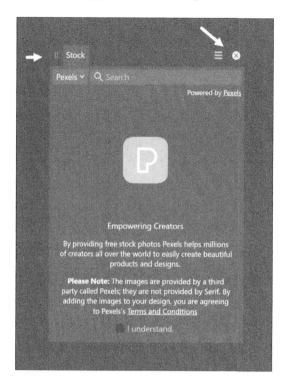

I can now click on that X in the top right corner to close it out.

If I instead wanted to reposition the panel, I could left-click and drag using the tab with the panel name (Stock in the image above) until the panel was positioned where I wanted it.

To dock a panel in a new location, you just drag it to a new dockable location, which we'll cover in a moment. Right now what we are going to do is build the workspace I want you to use for the rest of this book.

The first step is to remove the panels we don't need. That includes Stock on the top left side and Stroke on the top right side. I clicked and dragged them out and then used the X to close them rather than try to find them in the dropdown menu, but either way works.

Next, we need to move a few panels around.

On the top right side I prefer to have Layers, Character, Paragraph, Text Styles, and then Fields. I have nothing in the middle section. And then in the bottom right I put Transform, Text Frame, Swatches, and Color, but usually the only one down there I use for book layouts is Transform. You can also leave Navigator and History there if you want.

So we need to left-click on Character, Paragraph, and Text Styles and then drag to move each one up to the top right. We'll start with Character.

Left-click on the tab with the name and hold that left-click as you drag the panel into its new location. You should see the area flash blue first, but keep going until you see the tab next to any existing tabs. Like here where Character is now next to Layers and Color:

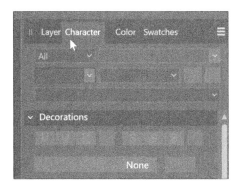

Release your left-click and that panel should now be one of the options in that row. (If you release the left-click when it flashes blue, that panel will be placed in its own row and not docked next to the other panel choices.)

Move the other two panels (Paragraph and Text Styles) into place using the same technique.

The reason I don't have a middle set of panels is because I like to be able to see my full list of layers and text styles without them cutting off because there's a panel below them. You'll see more of that in action later.

Next we need to add a few new panels that aren't available by default. Those are Find and Replace, Table of Contents, Index, and Preflight on the top left and Fields on the top right.

First, click on Pages, go to the Window option up top and then find each of those panels I listed for the top left.

Find and Replace is in the main menu and should insert right next to Pages. If it doesn't, drag the standalone panel into place so that it docks next to Pages. Repeat this with Table of Contents, Index, and Preflight. Table of Contents and Index are under the References secondary dropdown menu. Preflight is in the main dropdown.

For a basic title like we're going to create in this book, you won't use Table of Contents or Index, but this is my overall print set-up so I'm having you add them now. You don't have to if you don't want to. Index is for non-fiction.

Now click on the tab for Text Styles in the top right corner and then add

Fields which is in the References secondary dropdown menu.

For me, that one came in as an undocked panel, so I had to left-click and drag until it docked next to Text Styles.

For each section that contains panels, you will have only one panel visible at a time. So I can see only one of the Pages, Find and Replace, Table of Contents, Index, or Preflight panels at a time. Same with Layers, Character, Paragraph, Text Styles, or Fields. And with Transform, Swatches, Color, Navigator, and History.

My default is to have Pages, Layers, and Transform available and then to only click to the other panels as needed when working on a print layout.

Here is my final layout:

Since I also use Affinity Publisher to design covers and advertising images and I use very different panels when working on images, I like to save this layout so I can flip back and forth between my book layout workspace and my image workspace.

To do that you create a Studio Preset. This is also done under the Window option. Go to Window and then Studio, and choose Add Preset.

Click on that option to bring up the Add Preset dialogue box and type in the name you want to use:

Click OK to add that workspace layout (which they refer to as a studio) as a Studio Preset.

Affinity Publisher should default to the last layout you were using when you closed the program. To change to a different workspace layout, go to Window and then Studio and then choose the preset from the secondary dropdown menu:

Presets also will have a Ctrl shortcut assigned by default. The first one you create will be Ctrl + Shift + 1, the next one will be Ctrl + Shift + 2, etc.

If you ever decide that you need to rename a preset, you can do so by choosing Manage Studio Presets from that secondary dropdown menu. Click on the preset you want to rename and then the Rename option. This is also where you can go to delete an existing preset.

To change a preset, create your new workspace layout and then choose Add Preset, but give the preset the exact same name of your existing preset. Affinity will show a dialogue box that asks if you want to replace the existing studio preset. Say Yes and it will overwrite your former layout with the new one.

NEW FILE TEMPLATE

Okay. Now that we have our workspace set up, it's time to tell Affinity the type of document you want to create.

This is not going to be the same for every single person creating a print book. For example, my non-fiction computer books are 7.5 x 9.25 inches. My large print titles are 6 x 9 inches. And my regular paperbacks are 5.25 x 8 inches.

So you need to know starting off what size book you want to create. My advice is to look at books published by traditional publishers in your genre or subject area. You can usually see the book measurements listed on the book page on Amazon.

Also, make sure that you are looking at the right version of that book. For self-publishing most books are published in a trade format paperback size, which is the larger paperback. Don't look at the mass market paperback size.

If you're going to publish through Amazon's KDP program, be sure to choose a print size that is one of their listed sizes. You can find this by searching for Print Options under the Help function at their website. If you're going to do a hardcover version through them (only case-laminate style is available at this point in time), note that there is a much more limited selection of sizes available to you.

One thing to keep in mind with most print titles is that they use what's called mirrored margins. This means that the inner margins of two facing pages are the same size and the outer margins are the same size.

The inner margin is usually going to be bigger than the outer margin because there needs to be space for the pages to be bound into a book.

If you need to know what margins to use on a book and aren't sure, I'd recommend starting with the print templates provided by Amazon.

Okay. Once you've decided what size book you're going to create, you need to start that document in Affinity. Since we're already in the program, we can go to File and then choose New to bring up the New dialogue box. (Which I will note looks very different in Affinity Publisher 2.0 compared to the original program.)

Here it is:

You can see on the left-hand side that Affinity provides a number of pre-formatted options such as Letter, Legal, Business Card, and A4. These are listed under categories such as Print and Press Ready.

Scroll down and you'll see other categories listed, including Photo, Web, Devices, and Architectural. You can also create your own categories.

The dropdown menu at the very top will let you jump to a specific category or you can use the scroll bar on the right-hand side.

Each document listing also shows the basic dimensions for that document on the right-hand side of the listing. 148 mm x 210 mm for A5, for example.

Note at the bottom below the document listing you can also check or uncheck a box, "Show On Startup", to show this New dialogue box when you open Affinity Publisher.

The right-hand side of the dialogue box displays a sample two-page spread for the selected document, including any margins and bleed that have been set.

Below that are tabs for Layout, Pages, Color, Margins, and Bleed where you can specify those settings for that document.

Here we have an 8.5 x 11 inch document that is just a single page with the Layout tab selected.

None of the default documents are ever what I want. Which means I have to create my own. Since we're talking about print, I recommend starting with a template that is either set up for inches or set up for millimeters. You could technically start with any of the existing ones and then change the document units in the Layout tab, but the one time I tried that it did not go well. So I don't try to do that anymore.

Instead, I find a template that already has the correct units selected. In this case, I am going to start with the 8.5 x 11 inch option and then I'm going to change the dimensions in the Layout tab.

I want to change the width to 5.25 and the height to 8. Here we are:

For any book that has images in it, you will need a DPI of 300 or more. I usually set it to 305 to be safe. Also, you need to make a decision to either link to images wherever they're stored or to embed them.

If you embed images, that means that you'll potentially have a very large file size. But it also means that you never run into a situation where Affinity doesn't have the image to use in your document. It will warn you if that happens, but then you'll have to go find that image wherever it is and hope you have it. So for this book where we're just going to have one accent image, I'm going to choose to embed images. If this was non-fiction where I have a hundred-plus images in the book, I'd link my images instead.

Also, you can change this option later if needed. And Affinity will actually suggest that you do so if you work with too many embedded images.

Next, click over to the Pages tab. It should be facing pages, horizontally, start on right, and can have 1 page to start, which means we don't need to change anything here.

After that, click to the Color tab. For most basic print projects, you will want to have a black and white document. (Color is much more expensive to print.)

I use Gray/8 and Greyscale D50. If you are going to use color, then the choice you want here is CMYK not RGB. RGB is for colors on a screen not printed colors. If you're not sure what to use, check with your printer.

The next tab, Margins, is key. As I mentioned above, you can pull your margins from the KDP templates that Amazon offers. They are provided in Microsoft Word and you can go to Page Layout, Margins to see what values Amazon recommends. Combine the inside margin and gutter values to get your inside margin measurement if you do so.

For me for a 5.25 x 8 book, I use an inner margin of .9 inch, an outer margin of .6 inch, and then top and bottom margins of .76 inches which is what I pulled from an old Amazon template.

For large print I use 6 x 9 and my margins are 1 inch for the inner margin, .75 inch for the outer margin, and .9 inch for top and bottom.

I don't think you need bleed for a basic print book, but mine have it because I never changed it, so mine all have .125 inch bleed which seems to be the default value they use. (When you export it will normally export to PDF without the bleed. If you ever use Affinity Publisher to create a cover for your Amazon KDP print book then you will need to export with bleed.)

Okay, that's it. Our document layout is ready to go.

If you don't care to save these settings you can just click on Create. If you think you may want to use these settings to create another document at some point then you should make this document into a preset.

What I usually do is open the last book I formatted, delete out the contents, and then put in the new contents for my new title, so I don't need a preset for my print books, I just click on Create.

But let's walk through how to turn this into a preset, just in case.

At the top of the preview section of the New dialogue box, you'll see the title of the preset you're working with. If it's been edited, there will be a star next to the name, and you'll also be able to see a little box with a plus sign and also an update icon:

If you click on the update icon, that will overwrite the existing document template to reflect the changes you made.

If you click on the box with the plus sign, that will open the Create Preset dialogue box allowing you to keep the original template as-is but also create a new preset based upon your changes:

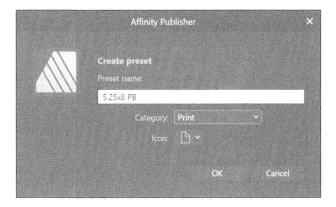

Type in the name you want, choose the category and icon, and then click on OK.

If you are not coming to Affinity Publisher 2.0 from the original Affinity Publisher and so didn't transfer over existing presets, then your category options will be limited to the default options of Print, Press Ready, etc.

To create a custom category, you can go to the very bottom of the preset listing on the left-hand side and click on the icon for Create Category. See here where the arrow is pointing at the option and then the Create Category dialogue box is shown:

If you create the category after you already created your preset, simply left-click on the preset and drag it down to the new category you created.

Once that preset is saved, make sure you have it selected, and click on Create to create your document. Affinity will then display that document in your workspace.

In our case what you're going to see is a single page of a document since we chose 1 for the number of pages for our default document:

The white space is the document page. The blue border within that white space shows where our specified margins are. The blue border outside the white space shows where the bleed border is.

The document is not actually formatted for text right now, it's just a blank slate, which you can see in the Pages panel which shows a blank page. (The Pages section of the Pages panel will always show how the document page would actually look if printed.) Those blue lines are just guidelines to follow when placing your elements.

Our next step is to create what are called Master Pages, which let us take this base and add elements like headers, footers, images, and text frames that remain constant across pages of that type.

Let's do that now. Don't worry, it will make more sense as we work through it.

MASTER PAGES

In my opinion, master pages are the core of what makes using Affinity Publisher so much better than using Word for print formatting.

Master pages are basically templates that you create that include your page numbering, your headers, your footers, any images you want on that type of page, and your text placement.

I create a master page for every type of two-page spread I need in a book, but you could also create one-page master pages, that's really up to you. Either way works. One-page master pages probably mean less chance of an error, but I find two-page master pages more intuitive to work with.

For a basic book like we're creating here, applying master pages is probably 75% of the formatting work. Text styles are the other big chunk of it.

We're going to create a total of nine master pages:

1. Title

2. Also By

3. Copyright and Chapter Start

4. No Text and Chapter Start

5. Text and Chapter Start

6. Text and Text

7. Chapter Start and Text

8. Text and About the Author

9. No Text and About the Author

Depending on where your text falls and the formatting choices you make, you may not need all of those. Or you may want to change them up. For example, you may prefer a Copyright and Also By page instead of a Copyright and Chapter Start page. But by the time we've built those nine master pages you should have the ability to create any master page you need.

If you were doing single-page master pages, then what you'd do is:

1. Title

2. Also By

3. Copyright

4. Chapter Start

5. Text

6. No Text

7. About the Author

We'll circle back to this when we create each of these, but if you're doing single-page master pages, be sure to use an alignment choice for your headers and footers that works on both left-hand and right-hand pages. Namely, you'll want to center your text or choose to align away from or towards the spine. (Usually not towards the spine, but it is an option.)

Okay. We're going to just dive in in a minute and create a few of these and it will start to make more sense, but first I want to work through a few high-level things related to master pages. (I'm assuming from this point forward that your workspace looks like mine. If it doesn't, adjust as needed.)

Go to the top left corner of your workspace where we placed the Pages panel and click on it.

You should see two sections, one for Master Pages and one for Pages. Click on Master Pages to expand that section. The panel should look like this once you do:

OPEN MASTER PAGE

Double-click on that Master A thumbnail in the Master Pages section to bring it up in the main workspace. Note that the master page has a left-hand and a right-hand page to it by default.

Whatever page or master page is in your main workspace is the one that can be edited at that point in time and the one that will show in the other panels.

RENAME MASTER PAGE

To rename a master page, click on the name under or next to its thumbnail in the Master Pages section of the Pages panel. A white box will appear around the name and the name will be highlighted in blue. Type in the new name you want and hit Enter.

ADD NEW MASTER PAGE

To add a new master page, right-click on an existing master page and choose Insert Master. This will bring up an Insert Master dialogue box where you can specify the name for the master page and any difference in dimensions or margins.

We will not change any of those settings in this book, so just type in the new master page name. If you do want to do one-page master pages instead of two-page master pages, click on Single instead of Facing in this dialogue box before creating the master page.

Another option is to right-click on a master page thumbnail and choose to Duplicate it. That will not only copy the page settings but any layers that have been placed onto that master page.

We will use the Duplicate option when creating our interior master pages to save time.

Be careful when you duplicate a master page, because by default Affinity will keep the first master page in the workspace. Which means you can end up making edits to the "wrong" master page. Always double-click on the thumbnail for the master page spread you want to edit just to be safe before you start making your edits to avoid this issue.

SEE MORE MASTER PAGES IN THE PAGES PANEL

If you're mostly working with master pages and you want to see more than just one at a time in the Pages panel, you can click on the Pages header in the panel to minimize the Pages section.

Here it is before I do that with both Master Pages and Pages expanded:

Here it is when I've minimized Pages and have the Master Pages section fully visible:

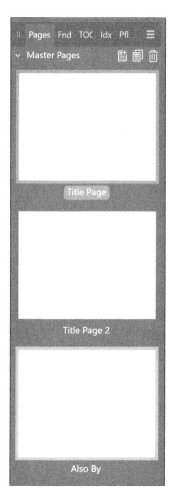

REARRANGE MASTER PAGES

To rearrange the order of your master pages in the Master Pages section, left-click and drag the thumbnail of the master page you want to move. Make sure that both pages are selected when moving a two-page master page and be sure to drag to the side of the other master page where you want to move it. You should see a blue line where it will move to.

I usually try to keep mine in order from start of the book to end of the book. So I'll have the Title master page at the top and the About the Author master page at the end. But you could do it alphabetically if that works better for you.

CHANGE THUMBNAIL SIZE IN PAGES PANEL

To change the size of the thumbnails in the Pages panel, left-click on the three lines at the end of the row with the panel tabs while you have the Pages panel selected:

Choose the thumbnail size you want. Small thumbnails will put the master page name to the side instead of below the thumbnail.

I prefer to use large thumbnails because it's easier to see the difference in the elements on each master page at a glance with a larger image.

DELETE A MASTER PAGE

To delete a master page, right-click on the thumbnail for the master page and choose Delete from the dropdown menu.

* * *

Okay. That's the basics of how to work with the Master Pages section of the Pages panel. Now let's go create our first master page, the Title Page.

TITLE MASTER PAGE

The Title page is going to be the first page in your document and will simply show the title and author for the book. Here is what the master page is going to look like when we're done:

It has two elements, the text frame where we can enter the book title and the accent image. For each master page you want to include the elements that will *always* appear on that page, which is why this master page does not include any text.

Also, remember that I'm doing a very simple layout here. You can obviously take what we do and fancy it up as much as you want later. This is one way of doing things, not the only way.

To get started, go to the Master Pages section of the Pages panel and rename the first thumbnail Title Page.

(For a new document there should only be the one thumbnail, but if you added master pages in the last chapter and didn't later delete them you may have more than one.)

Next, double-click on that thumbnail. Your workspace should look something like this:

As I mentioned before, those blue borders do not appear in the final printed document. They are just there to let you know where to place the various elements.

They also do not constrain any text or images that you add. So if you typed text directly onto this page, it would go right across those blue lines without a problem.

To constrain text to a specific area, you need to use a text frame. So let's do that now.

Our text is going to go on the right-hand page and needs to fall somewhere within the blue rectangle visible on the white space on that page. I don't want the text to start that high though, so I'm going to place a text frame that is the same width as the blue rectangle but not as tall.

To add a text frame we use the Frame Text Tool which is on the left-hand side at the top of the list of tools. It looks like a T in a square and you can see its name if you hold your mouse over it like I've done here:

Click on that icon and then left-click and drag in the main workspace to create your frame. As you left-click and drag you'll see a blue frame appear in the workspace, like this:

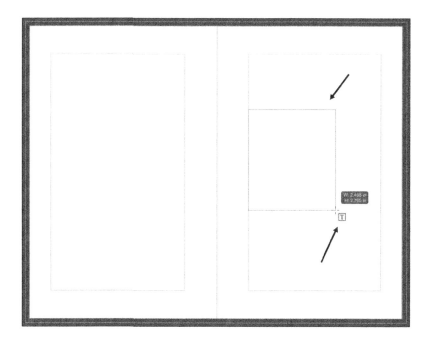

You can see that I'm using the Frame Text Tool because my cursor is that T in a box and you can see the outline of the frame that I'm creating there in the middle of the right-hand page.

I want this frame to line up with the edges of the available space we set for our text in the document setup stage, so I am going to keep dragging the edges of that text frame until it aligns with both sides and the bottom of that original blue rectangle.

But let's say I stopped too soon so I just have this text frame that is too small for what I want.

I can click on the text frame and then left-click on any of the white circles around the perimeter or in the corners and hold that left-click as I drag to resize the frame to what I need.

When you reach the blue rectangle with your text frame, you will see either a green or red line appear. If the frame is aligned with the lines on the sides, the line you see will be green. If it's aligned on the top or bottom, the line will be red.

You can see both here as well as a green line through the center that indicates the text frame is centered left-to-right to that blue rectangle:

The alignment lines also extend off of the page. This is probably a little hard to see in the black and white print version because you won't see the colors of the lines, but you can still see a horizontal line there at the bottom that extends off the page to both sides as well as three vertical lines that extend off the top and bottom of the page.

When you see the green and red lines that means that your text frame border is aligned with the blue rectangle that outlines where your text can go.

These alignment lines will actually appear for all elements on a page as we'll see later, so for a more complex layout you'd need to be a little more careful that it's aligned to the correct element, but for now this works just fine.

If you're not seeing those red and green lines, that's because they only appear when Snapping is enabled.

It looks like it is the default in Affinity Publisher 2.0 for Snapping to be enabled, but if it isn't for you, then go to the middle of the options menu up top and find the image that looks like a horseshoe-shaped magnet. (If you hold your mouse over it, it will say Snapping.)

Click on the dropdown arrow next to the image and make sure that the Enable Snapping box at the top left is checked:

Snapping is something that I leave on at all times because it is often the easiest way to align the various elements in your document. If, however, you find it annoying you can also go there to uncheck that box and turn it off as needed.

Okay. So insert your text frame, keeping in mind that the top of the *text frame* is where your title text will start. Here's mine:

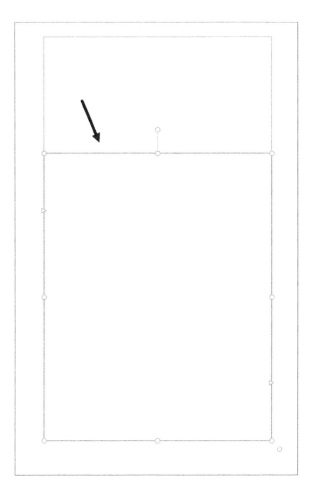

I've clicked on the text frame so you can see its outline by looking at the little circles around the perimeter. It overlaps with the blue rectangle from our document setup on three sides, but is not as tall as that rectangle.

Now let's add an image. (You can skip ahead if you don't want to use one, but I want to show you how this works.)

I find that simple images that use solid colors work best for something like this, because they easily translate to black and white. Here, I have a number that I can choose from courtesy of Design Cuts packages I've bought over the years (https://www.designcuts.com/):

Any of these could probably work, the question would be where to position them relative to the text to make it look "good". No guarantee I'm going to pull that off here, but I will at least show you the how of it.

Be sure if you do use an image in your book design that you have the rights to do so. The Design Cuts packages come with commercial rights. Depositphotos and Shutterstock are two other places I've bought images in the past.

(Also, you want the image you use to be a high enough resolution so that it prints at 300 DPI or more when printed in its final size. That shouldn't be an issue if you buy the image from a professional site, but could be if you try to use a personal photo or an image you saved from a website since most websites or images viewed on a computer look fine at a lower resolution.)

We're going to place this image directly onto the document. (The other option would be to use a picture frame, which is covered in the next book in this series.)

To place the image, first click on the black arrow on the top left of the workspace. This is the Move Tool and it will get you away from using the Frame Text Tool.

Next, click on the Place Image Tool option on the left-hand side, which looks like a drawing of mountains:

That is going to bring up the Open dialogue box. Navigate to where you have your picture saved, select it, and then choose Open.

Your cursor will now look like a fat white arrow with another arrow pointing down at a bluish-colored oval:

Move the cursor to where you want to place the image and left-click and drag until the image is the size you want. When you let up on the left-click you will have your image in your document surrounded by a border.

Don't worry too much about getting the placement or size exactly right, just get it close to where you want it initially.

If you already clicked on the Move Tool before you started, you can then left-click anywhere on the image and drag it into position.

Here I have placed the image so that the right edge is aligned to the right edge of the text frame and the center of the image is aligned to the top of the text frame:

In the ebook and color versions of this book you'll see that those lines are green and red to show the alignment. In the black and white version they should be darker.

If you don't like the size of the image, you can either left-click and drag from the corner of the image to change its size, or you can change the image dimensions in the Transform panel by adjusting the W or H (width or height) values.

Remember that we placed the Transform panel in the bottom right corner.

If you use the Transform panel to change an image, be sure to lock the aspect ratio so that both the width and height will change at the same time so that the image stays proportionate.

You do this by clicking on the little "lock" image to the right of the width and height values before you change either one. Hold your mouse over it and you'll see that it's the Lock Aspect Ratio option:

If you somehow change an image so that it is not in the proportions it was when you imported it, Affinity will warn you about this in the Preflight panel. You can see here that I stretched this image sideways without also adjusting its height:

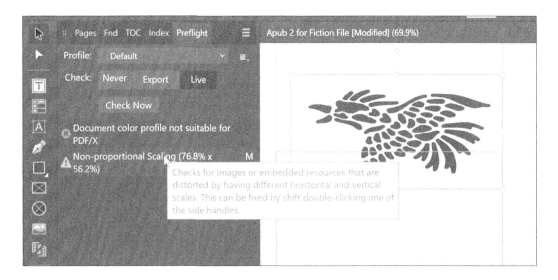

The second noted item in the Preflight panel is telling me that. I've placed my mouse over the warning so you can also see what it means and how Affinity tells you to fix it.

To fix it, hold down the Shift key and then double-click on one of the circles on the side of the image to get the image back to proportional scaling. Be careful, though, because that might make the image a size you don't want to use and you'll then have to resize again. But it does at least fix the image proportions quickly.

Okay. So. Import your image and then position it where you want it relative to your text frame and the margins of your document.

I prefer not to let my images overflow into the margins. You can, though, it's not forbidden. But if you allow the image to go all the way to the edge of the page, I believe you then need to choose a different bleed option when you publish and would need to extend it past the white space to where the bleed border is.

Here is our final Title Page master page with the Pages and Layers panels visible:

You can see in the Master Pages section of the Pages panel which elements of the document will actually display when this page is exported. Namely, just the image we inserted. The text frame will not be visible nor are the outlines that show where the margins are.

In the Pages section, you can see that because this is the first page of our document and it starts on the right-hand side that only the right-hand side of this master page will show in the final document.

Also, if you look to the Layers panel, which was visible in the screenshot at the start of this chapter, you will see that we have added two elements to this master page. One is the image and one is the text frame.

Now let's go down to the Pages section of the Pages panel and bring up our actual document so we can add our book title and see how that works because we have one more tweak to make here to finalize this master page.

ADD TITLE PAGE TO DOCUMENT

By default, because we only have the one master page, Affinity will use that master page for the document that's shown in the Pages section of the Pages panel which is only one page long at this point.

To open and edit that page, go to the Pages section of the Pages panel and double-click on its thumbnail. This will bring up the page in the main workspace.

This is where you want to add your title text. Not in the Master Pages section, but in the Pages section.

To do that, click on the Artistic Text Tool which is an A in a box, two below the Frame Text Tool:

Next, click into the text frame in your document and start typing:

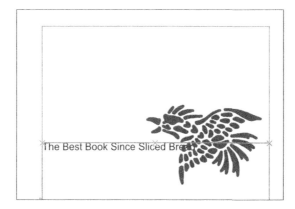

Here I have typed "The Best Book Since Sliced Bread" and you can see that the text appears at the top of that text frame.

I don't like the font or font size, though. And we also need to deal with the issue of the text disappearing behind the image. Let's deal with the font first.

Use Ctrl + A to select all of the text you just typed. It should highlight that text in blue. You could also select the text using a left-click and drag or using Shift and the arrow keys.

Next, go to the dynamic menu up top (it changes depending on which tool is currently in use). There should be three dropdowns there as well as buttons to select for bold, italics, and underline:

The first dropdown is for font. It lets you choose a font to use:

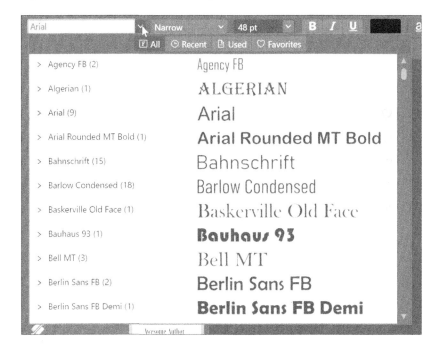

If you have a particular font in mind, click into the field that displays the current font name and start typing the font name you want. The dropdown menu will shift to that part of the listing and you can then click on the font name.

If you're not sure, you can see what each font looks like because each entry is written in that font. Note the difference between Algerian, Arial, Bahnschrift, and Bauhaus 93 in this list, for example. Also, as you put your mouse over each of the fonts in the list the selected text in your document will temporarily change to show how that font will look when applied to that text.

Which fonts are available is going to depend on you and which fonts you have loaded onto your computer. Thanks to Design Cuts I have a lot of fonts that I can use. If you haven't purchased fonts, be careful with licensing issues. It's possible you have a font on your computer for "personal" use with Microsoft programs but really shouldn't be using it for commercial design projects. I believe you're safe for the interior of a book but not the cover, but I am not a lawyer so you'll want to research that more thoroughly (or just buy the font you're going to use so it's not an issue).

You can click on the heart icon next to a font to favorite the font. If you do that, then the Favorites tab at the top of the font listing will include it.

You can also click on the Recent or Used tabs at the top of the font listing to see the fonts you've used recently or that have been used in the document at some point.

The next dropdown menu shows the various options you have for that font. It will include any available weights (light, regular, medium, bold, etc.), any italic versions, as well as expanded or condensed versions.

Here you can see that for Arial:

It turns out (and maybe you already know this), but the "bold" version of a font and the "italic" version of a font and the "bold italic" version of a font are all separate files, so you're only going to have those options for a font if you have those specific files loaded on your computer.

In this case, I have regular, (regular) italic, (regular) bold, (regular) bold italic, and also narrow versions of each.

Because I have those options available for the Regular weight that I have selected in the dropdown above, the Bold and Italic buttons are also available for me to click on. (That's the B and the slanted I visible at the end of that same row in the screenshot.)

But for other fonts, like Jupiter here, I don't have all of those options:

You can see that Jupiter only comes in Regular and Bold. Since there is not an italic version, the slanted I is grayed out.

Finally, the third dropdown there is for the size of your font. The larger the number, the larger the text. You can also type in a value.

If you have text selected, as you place your cursor over a font, font weight, or font size, that text in your document will change to show your selection, but you need to click on the option to apply it.

These same options are also available at the top of the Character panel if you want to use that instead.

I made my changes and here is what I ended up with:

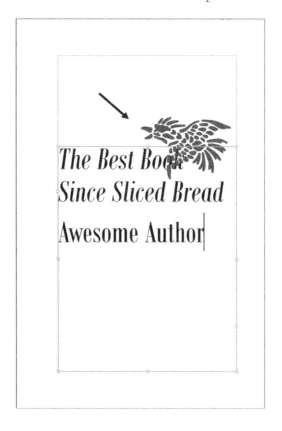

I went with 48 pt Bodoni MT. I used Condensed Italic for the title and just Condensed for the author name.

But you can see that we have a problem. Because the word "book" is running into that image.

We need to tell Affinity to not let that happen. The way you do that is by changing one of the settings for the *image*, which means we need to go back to the master page.

Double-click on the thumbnail for that master page. Go to the Layers panel and click on the layer for the image or click on the image directly in the document.

Once you do that, in the top menu there should be an option for Show Text Wrap Settings (see the screenshot below).

Click on that to bring up the Text Wrap dialogue box:

The setting we want to use here is Tight and then Largest Side. This will make sure that any text is kept to the left of our image (the larger side) and that it wraps to the next line as soon as it reaches the point where it would touch the image.

As soon as I made those two selections and closed the dialogue box, the change was reflected on the title page in my document:

You can see that "book" is now on the second line and that "sliced" also moved to the next line to avoid overlapping with the bird's wing.

That wrap text setting will hold for any other page in the document that uses this master page so it only needs to be set once per master page.

Okay. Next let's do the Also By master page.

ALSO BY MASTER PAGE

The Also By master page is where you can list other titles by that author if there are any. We're going to create one that's very simple and has a text frame on the right-hand page as well as our accent image. It should look like this when it's done:

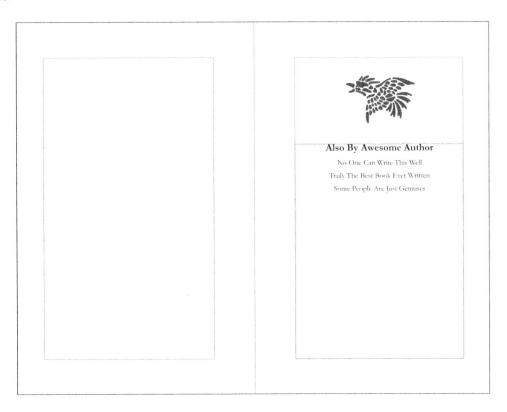

First, we need another master page to work on.

I'm just going to be lazy here and duplicate the Title master page since it already has the two elements we need, a text frame and accent image.

To do that, right-click on the thumbnail for the Title master page and select Duplicate from the dropdown menu.

Scroll down (if needed) to see the new master page. Rename it.

Finally, double-click on that thumbnail to make sure the master page in the main workspace is the correct one.

Because I duplicated the title page, I already have a text frame and an image to work with, so all I have to do is resize or reposition them as needed. And because the Also By text should be consistent across all books in the series, I can add the text into the master page. That will save me effort with later books in the series.

I want to experiment a bit to see what works here. First, I'm going to try making the text start closer to the top of the page. To do that, I need to resize the text frame.

First step is to make sure the Move Tool is selected. That's the black arrow at the top of the left-hand set of icons.

Next, I can either go to the Layers panel and click on the Frame Text layer there, or I can click directly on the text frame in my master page. I usually choose to use the Layers panel.

Once I've done that I just left-click and drag from the blue circle at the top of the frame until I've changed the height to what I want.

Okay. So I did that.

Next, I want to make the image smaller, so I click on the image layer. I can then either use the Transform panel (making sure the aspect ratio is locked) or left-click and drag from one of the corners of the image to resize it.

Once I've changed the image size I need text to really see if this works. So I click on the Artistic Text Tool and then click into the text frame and add the titles I want to list. While I'm there I want to make sure the font is the same as I used on the Title master page, Bodoni MT.

Here we go:

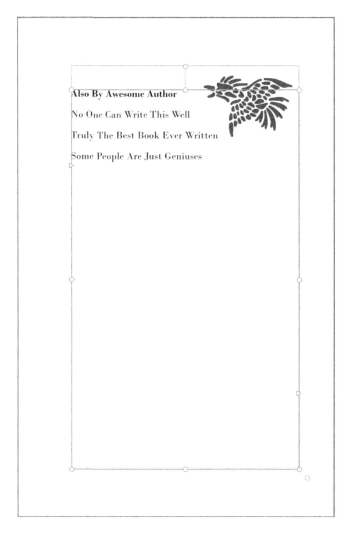

I don't like it. Left-aligned was fine for the title page, but I want this text centered. And actually, given the number of titles I think the text starts too high on the page.

If I'm going to bring that text back down, then it makes sense to have the text frame be the same height as the title page. So let's go back to the Title master page real quick and click on the text frame and then look at the Transform panel:

I want my text frame on my Also By master page to use all of these values. X and Y show where on the page the text frame is located, W and H set its size. I don't have to change all four values, though, just H and Y.

So let me do that. I take the H and Y values from the Title master page and apply them to the text frame on the Also By master page. Now I have a text frame that is the exact same height as the prior page.

Another way I could've done this was to delete the text frame on the Also By master page, go to the Title master page, click on the text frame layer, use Ctrl + C to copy it, go back to the Also By master page and click on it, and then use Ctrl + V to paste the text frame I copied.

Often that will put the copied element into the exact same location on the new master page.

Or I could've just undone (Ctrl + Z) my changes on the Also By master page until I was back to the original version which was a copy of the Title master page.

But since I'd already typed in text, using the Transform panel seemed like the easiest option.

Now that I've changed the text frame height, that creates a lot of white space at the top of the page, so I think I'm going to center the image this time. To do that, I just left-click on the image and drag until the image is centered in that white space above the text frame but still within the blue rectangle that shows where text should go.

If you ever center an image in a print layout using the Snapping lines, be sure that you're centering to the blue rectangle that shows where text should be as opposed to the whole page. Remember that we have uneven margins to allow for the fact that the inner margin also needs space for binding the pages, which means that the center of the page will not be the same as the center of the area where your text goes.

Usually Affinity will show both lines if you move the image around. You want the outer center line, not the inner one.

Okay. If we're going to center the image, then we also need to center the text.

(It's currently left-aligned.)

To do that, we can select the text and then use the dynamic menu up top. The text alignment options are towards the right-hand side of that menu:

The first option, which is currently selected, is Align Left, next to that is Align Center, followed by Align Right, and then a dropdown of additional options.

Above I have my cursor over the Align Center option so you can see the description. I can just click on that to apply it.

If you don't want to use the dynamic menu, you can also go to the top of the Paragraph panel to find those same alignment options, as well as the ones in the dropdown menu:

And here we go:

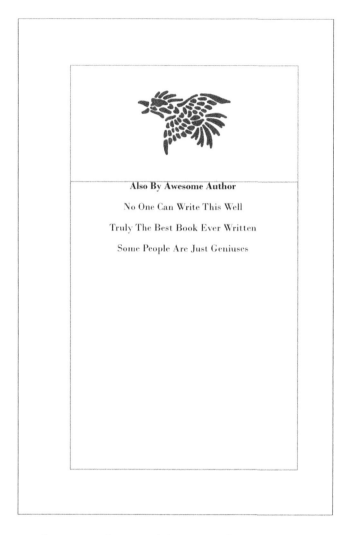

A centered image and centered text with a text frame that matches the title page. That works for me.

* * *

Now let's add the Also By page spread to our document.

First step is to go to the Pages section of the Pages panel, right click on the thumbnail there, and choose Add Pages.

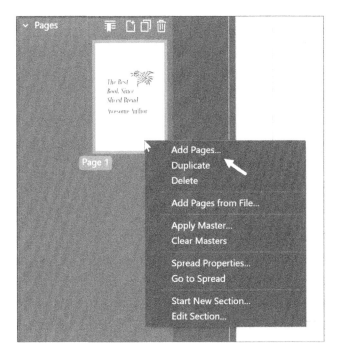

This will open the Add Pages dialogue box. We want to add 2 pages, After the page we just right-clicked on, and we want to change the Master Page dropdown menu to Also By:

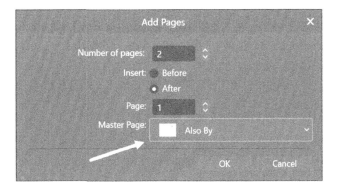

Then we click OK and now in our Pages section, which shows the actual pages of our document, we have our next two pages:

Done. We have a three-page document with a title page and an also by page.

* * *

A quick caution.

If you put text on the master page, like we did here, that's where you should then edit that text.

It can be easy to forget where the text was originally added and to then make changes in the document instead of the master page. But if you do that, then any changes you make to that master page will not carry through to the document.

For example, I just edited the font on the Also By master page. When I hadn't touched the text used on that page in my main document, the font change immediately carried through. But when I had made a change to that text in the main document, the font change did not carry through.

That may sound confusing. You'll understand what I'm talking about if you ever end up making that mistake. I usually run into it with the copyright box that we're about to create.

Basically, if something is on a master page, best practice is to edit it there even if you can edit it in the main document.

COPYRIGHT AND CHAPTER START
MASTER PAGE

Those were both very simple master pages that only had two elements. Now we're going to create a slightly more complex master page, the Copyright and Chapter Start master page, which uses text frames on both pages and also includes a footer with the page number:

First step, go to the Master Pages section of the Pages panel and Duplicate the Also By master page. Rename it. Double-click on the thumbnail to be sure that you're on the correct master page.

Next, delete the Also By text but leave the text frame and the image. Also, click into the text frame and change the alignment back to Align Left.

Now we need to look at that text frame on the right-hand page and decide if it needs to be adjusted.

Most chapters in books do not start at the top of the page. It does sometimes happen, but that's the exception more than the rule.

Also, the first time I created a Chapter Start master page in Affinity I created a separate text frame for the chapter title. You could do that, and some of the books in my sample stack on my desk probably did. But it's a lot more effort to do things that way.

Better, in my opinion, when you're just starting out, to set apart your chapter titles using a different font choice, size, and/or alignment. That's what we're going to do here.

Which means that the top of the text frame at the beginning of a Chapter Start page is going to be where the chapter title is shown. The actual text of that chapter will fall somewhere below that.

(You'll see this in action in a bit.)

So the question is, do we think that the text frame as it exists right now is low enough on the page to indicate a chapter start, but also high enough on the page to accommodate a chapter title, and still have the text start at a reasonable point on the page?

For now, I think so. But I may change my mind later when we come up with our chapter title format and drop in the text.

I also think that the placement of the accent image will work for a chapter start, so we can leave that alone as well. (This is why we copied the Also By master page, since those elements were already in a good position for us to reuse.)

Which means all we need to add to this master page is the copyright text and the footer.

Let's do the copyright text first. Click on the Frame Text Tool and then click and drag to place a text frame in the bottom left portion of the text area on the left-hand page. If you have a lot of text that you want to include for your copyright notice, make the text frame tall enough to accommodate it. For me it's usually just a few short lines so I keep my text frame small.

Next, add the copyright text you want to use into the text frame.

I put "Copyright © XXXX Author Name, All Rights Reserved, ISBN: XXXXXX" where those commas are line breaks. I include the XXXX placeholders for the copyright year and ISBN number so I won't forget to update them later:

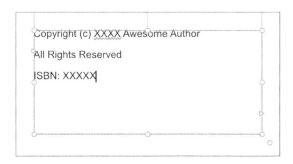

But keep in mind that doing it that way means that you will need to edit this text at some point. I always edit it in the document not in the master page, which means any other changes I make on this master page after I do that won't carry forward to the actual document.

I'm comfortable with that because once I have a template set up I generally don't need to touch my existing master pages, so there are no edits to font, etc. that I need to worry about.

Also, ISBN and copyright year are the very last information I add to a document before finalizing it. That means I should have already caught and fixed any formatting issues with my master pages by that point.

Next step is to use Ctrl + A to select all of that text and change the font and, if wanted, the font size. I always put my copyright notice in the same font I'm going to use for the main body text.

For a regular print book you will want to use some sort of serifed font. Serifed fonts are ones that have little feet at the bottom of letters like "m". I often use Garamond. Times New Roman is another safe choice. If you read a book and really like the font, sometimes they'll have a little paragraph somewhere in the backmatter that tells you what font they used.

For large print I use a sans-serif font called Verdana that is supposedly easier to read for someone who is sight-impaired. There are about a half dozen fonts out there that are recommended for large print. If you're going to go that route, I recommend researching it and making your own decision.

Ideally, your layout would have only one serifed font. That would mean your main body text, headers, etc. would be in that font and then you'd use a non-serifed, script, or decorative font for your chapter headers or other design elements.

For now, I'm going to break that rule since I already started with Bodoni for the title page and also by text. I suspect it wouldn't work for the main body so I'm going to use Garamond for that.

(All design experts are screaming in horror at this moment. The joys and dangers of self-publishing are that you can do anything you want.)

Getting back to our copyright notice. I'm changing the font to Garamond, Regular, 12 pt, and centering the text.

Now that we've chosen our font, we need to fix the copyright symbol. I wrote it as (c) and it stayed that way, which means I now need to go replace that with the appropriate glyph. To do so, highlight the (c) and go to Window→Text →Glyph Browser. That will bring up the Glyph Browser panel:

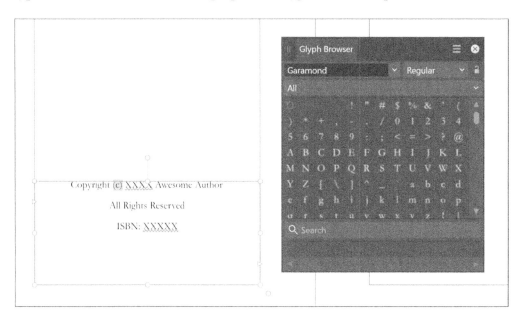

It should already be on the correct font (Garamond, Regular in my case). Scroll down until you find the copyright symbol written in that font and double-click on it. That will insert the symbol in place of your selected text.

Close the glyph browser.

While we're here, I also want to change the default spacing between those lines of text. Select the text and then go to the Paragraph panel in the top right and change the value for Leading at the top in the Spacing section. I changed mine to 14 point.

Next, we need a footer so we can include a page number for the chapter start page.

First step, click on the Frame Text Tool and insert a text frame on the bottom of the right-hand page in the margin area. I always make mine the same width as the text frame for the main text. Also, make sure it's tall enough to display your text in your chosen font size.

I also usually put it a little bit away from the main text frame, but not too close to the bottom of the page.

Click into the text frame and then go to the top menu and choose Text →Insert→Fields→Page Number.

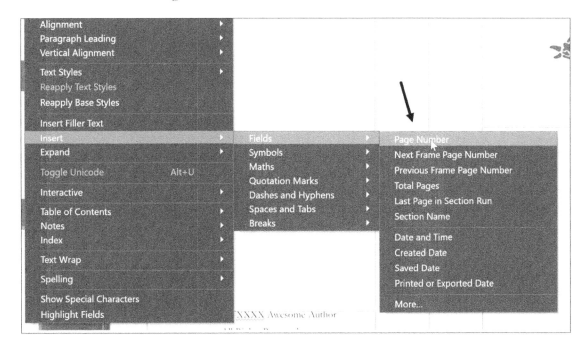

Affinity will insert a # sign into that text frame, which is the placeholder for the page number. Select All (Ctrl + A) and center the text. It should already be in Garamond, Regular, 12 point. If you want to use some other font, weight, or size, you could change that now.

If you prefer to have your page numbers on the outer edge of the page, which is recommended for large print, then the option you want to use is Align Away From Spine, which is in the dropdown menu in the dynamic menu at the top, or is the last option in the Paragraph panel row of icons.

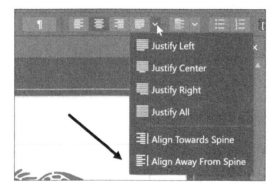

You don't want to use left or right alignment here, because that won't work on both the right- and left-hand pages. Choosing align away from spine saves a little effort and lets you just copy the footer when we move on to master pages that have the page number on both the left-hand and right-hand pages.

For me that's not a concern because I chose to center the page number.

I am also going to align the text in the text frame to the center of the frame top to bottom which is called Center Vertically.

The option is available in a dropdown to the right of the left, center, right, etc. options:

I do this because I have run into issues with documents that use picture frames and images where the text in my footer was impacted by the existence of those frames so that a right-hand page number didn't line up with a left-hand page number. Aligning the text to the center of the text frame fixed that issue.

Okay. Here we go:

Copyright © XXXX Awesome Author
All Rights Reserved
ISBN: XXXXX

We have our accent image. It's above our text frame where our main text will go. There's a text frame on the left-hand page that includes our copyright notice. And for the main body of the document we have a footer that includes a page number.

In the original version of this book I also showed my footer using accent images on either side of that number. You can insert those either using the glyph browser or by using a different font that has images available. This time around I'm just going to keep the footer simple.

The one thing I would suggest you don't try, because I have done this and it turned out to be annoying, is insert images in that footer text frame. You can do it. I did do it. But it was more trouble than it was worth.

Okay. On to the next master page. Let's do the No Text and Chapter Start page, because it's really easy to do from this point.

NO TEXT AND CHAPTER START
MASTER PAGE

For a novel, you will probably not need this master page. If you flip through most traditionally-published novels you'll see that the chapters generally start on whichever page is next. So sometimes the chapter starts on the left, sometimes on the right. There are no blank pages once things get going.

Where a No Text and Chapter Start master page is used is for non-fiction or short story collections. In both of those cases, it's more likely that each section, chapter, or story will start on the right-hand page. If there's not enough text to naturally make that happen, then you need a blank left-hand page to force it to happen.

So let's create that now.

Go to the Master Pages section of the Pages panel, Duplicate the Copyright and Chapter Start master page, rename it to No Text and Chapter Start, and then double-click on the thumbnail.

Next, go to the Layers panel, right-click on the text frame layer that is for the copyright notice, and choose Delete to remove that layer:

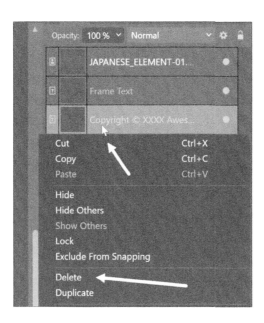

You can also click on that layer in the Layers panel and use the Delete key on your computer, at least on a PC.

Or you could choose the Move Tool and then click on the copyright text frame in your main workspace and use Delete, right-click and choose Cut, or use Ctrl + X.

Be sure if you try to do this directly in the document that the Move Tool is selected or you may end up deleting text instead of the text frame.

And there you have it:

Nothing on the left-hand page and a chapter start on the right-hand page. Easy peasy.

Alright, let's go ahead and create the rest of our master pages right now. It will feel like we're not doing much of anything, but what we're doing here is putting in place the framework that makes the rest of formatting a book much, much, much easier. So just stick with me on this.

TEXT AND CHAPTER START MASTER PAGE

The next master page we're going to create is the Text and Chapter Start master page. First, go to the Master Pages section of the Pages panel, Duplicate the No Text and Chapter Start master page, rename it, and double-click on the thumbnail to make sure it's the one showing in the main workspace. (You may at this point need to scroll down to find that thumbnail image in your Master Pages section.)

The right-hand page is already set up, so all we need to do is set up the left-hand page. That requires a header, a text frame, and a footer.

Let's start with the footer. Make sure the Move Tool (black arrow) is selected. Click on the footer on the right-hand page, use Ctrl + C to copy and Ctrl + V to paste, and then left-click and drag that copied footer over to the left-hand page and make sure that it lines up with the footer on the right-hand page as well as the text area on the left-hand page.

Like so:

In the ebook or color edition you should be able to see the red and green lines that show that the new footer is aligned with the old one and the text area on the left-hand page. In the black and white print version you should see dark lines that show that alignment.

That's the footer. Easy enough.

Now let's put in our text frame. And I'll tell you why we're doing it in this order in a moment. So, click on the Frame Text Tool (the capital T), and then left-click and drag to create a text frame that fills the entire available space for text on the left-hand page, so overlaps the blue rectangle that's already there.

You can see above that my text frame is the same size and shape as the blue border underneath. If you do this right you'll only see one rectangle, but it will have the circles visible around the perimeter indicating that you're seeing a text frame.

Next, we need the header. Click on the Move Tool, click on the footer on the left-hand page, and then use Ctrl + C to copy and Ctrl + V to paste. (You can also right-click and choose Copy and Paste that way, but control shortcuts are quicker. If you're on a Mac, I believe you use Cmd.)

What I want you to do next is arrow up and then back down once and I want you to notice the value that Affinity displays above the text frame for the footer.

Here, for example, that is .174:

That number represents the distance from the top of the footer to the text frame where the main text will display. We want the header to be that same distance from the text. Or at least, that's how I like to do it.

Once you know that number, you can left-click and drag the copied footer up into the header area of the left-hand page and then position it so that the header is aligned to the text frame for the main body text and is the same distance above that frame as the footer is below it. I do this by aligning it on the left and right edges first and then using the up and down arrows to get that distance.

In this case I was able to get .173 above, which is close enough.

Once the header is in position, we need to change the contents. Right now it shows the page number, which needs to be removed, and we need to replace that with author name. Click on the Artistic Text Tool (the capital A), click into the frame, delete the # sign, and then go to the Fields panel, which we placed in the top right corner at the end.

Click on the space next to Author and it should turn white:

Type in the author name you want to use for the document and hit Enter. Double-click on the white text that says Author to the left of that. This will insert your author name into the header on your master page. (I wish it inserted as a field name <Author>, so you'd understand that this is a field and not text that was manually entered, but it doesn't.)

And, here you go:

One Text and Chapter Start master page. But we have one more thing we need to do. And that's tell Affinity that the text from the left-hand page should flow to the right-hand page. This master page is for where a chapter ends and the next chapter starts and we're going to put our entire book into Affinity at once so we need our chapters to connect to one another.

The way to do this is to click on the left-hand text frame. When you do that, you'll see a very small blue arrow on the right-hand side of the frame.

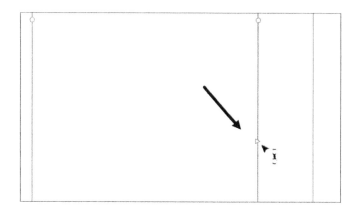

Click on that arrow and it will shade the entire text frame blue. Move your cursor over to the right-hand text frame, which will then also shade in blue:

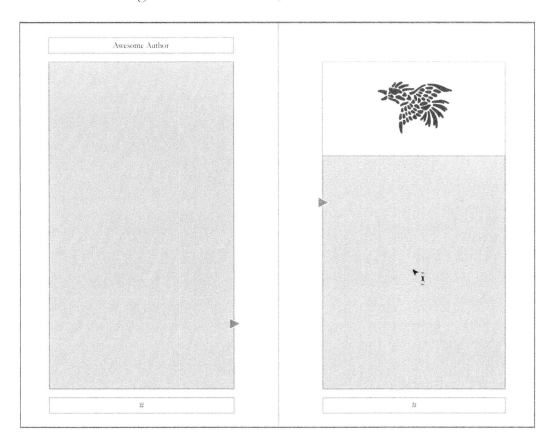

Click on the second text frame. You should now see a line that connects the two text frames with an arrow on that line pointing in the direction of the right-hand text frame. That indicates the direction the text will flow.

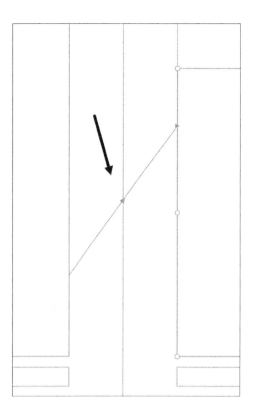

And now we're done with this one.

* * *

Quick note, Affinity is really good in my experience at generating recovery files, so if it ever crashes on you try to reopen the file you had open at the time and it will often have the file saved almost up to the moment it crashed. But I also currently have a pretty, shiny, new piece of you-know-what computer that randomly crashes on me a lot so I also recommend using Ctrl + S or saving regularly as you work on a project like this, just in case.

Second quick note, while we're taking a break here. The headers and footers I'm showing you in this book are one acceptable option. I wanted you to have a version that uses headers and footers so you could work with those. But you can do whatever you want.

I currently have six fiction titles sitting on my desk. (I read a lot and am too lazy to put things away.) Four of those titles have page number on the top outer edge of each page with author name on the left center top and title on the right center top of the page. So no footer. One has title on the left top, author on the right top, and page numbers on the bottom, all centered. The final one just has page numbers centered on the bottom and no title or author at all.

Those are all recent fiction books published by traditional publishers. The ones that don't have both a header and a footer probably did fit more text on those pages and cut down on number of pages printed by a small amount, so it may be worth experimenting with if that's a big concern for you.

At least when we're done here you should know enough about how to do these that you can configure it any way you want. Okay, on to the next.

TEXT AND TEXT MASTER PAGE

Our next master page is the Text and Text master page. This is the bread and butter of your book. Most of your book will likely be text and text pages, unless you have really short chapters (like I sometimes do).

First step, Duplicate the Text and Chapter Start master page that we just created and rename it. Double-click to make sure you have the right pages showing in the main workspace. (And, yes, I'm going to say that every time because of the number of times I have personally messed that up.)

Step one, delete the image. I did so using the Layers panel and the Delete key after I clicked on that layer.

Step two, click on the text frame for the right-hand page and click and drag the circle on the top of the frame until the text frame fills the entire space allowed for text, so overlaps the blue rectangle completely.

Step three, click on, copy, paste, and move the header from the left-hand page to the right-hand page until it is aligned with the text frame and the left-hand header.

If that doesn't work—in my case the header did not want to show alignment lines to the left-hand header—check the Transform panel value for the left-hand header to see the Y value and then change the Y value for the right-hand header to match.

Next, click onto the Artistic Text Tool and then into the frame for the right-hand header and delete the text there. Once that text is gone, go to the Fields panel and double-click on the white text that says Title. It will insert the title of your document into that header.

If you want the title to be different, click on the text for the title in the Fields panel and change it. The document will update automatically.

Be careful with long titles to make sure that they fit into the header text frame.

Finally, confirm that there is text flow from the left-hand page to the right-hand page. If not, connect the two text frames by clicking on the left-hand text frame, clicking on the blue arrow along the right-hand edge, and then clicking on the right-hand text frame.

When you're done you should have something that looks like this:
There are two text frames, a header on each page, a footer on each page, and the text will flow from the left-hand page to the right-hand page.

CHAPTER START AND TEXT MASTER PAGE

Now we need a master page for when a chapter starts on the left-hand side of the page. This is one that you'll want for most fiction books, but generally not need for non-fiction or short story collections.

For this one, go and Duplicate the Text and Chapter Start master page. Rename it. Double-click on the thumbnail.

The first thing we're going to do here is to insert the header on the right-hand page. There are a number of ways to do this. I am going to go to the Text and Text master page, copy the header on the right-hand page there, and then paste on this new master page. That pasted my header right where it needed to be and it had the book title already there.

That usually will work. But I've had it not work at times. Maybe because I didn't have the Move Tool selected, I don't know. If that option doesn't work, you can also duplicate the left-hand header, move the copy over, and then make sure the Y value matches up for both headers before deleting the left-hand one. You'd then also need to change the Author field and replace it with the Title field.

You could also just note the Y value for the left-hand header before dragging that header over to the right-hand page so you don't have to go back and delete anything.

Any of those options will work.

Next step, delete the left-hand header if it's still there. I click on it in the document and then go to the Layers panel and right-click and choose Delete from there.

Now we need to change our text frames. Click on the right-hand text frame and jot down the H and Y values in the Transform panel. Now click on the left-hand text frame and change the H and Y values in the Transform panel to match.

In this case, make sure that lock aspect ratio is NOT turned on so that the W value remains unchanged.

You should now have short text frames on both the left-hand and right-hand page and they should both be lined up along the bottom of the blue rectangle.

Move the image from the right-hand page to the left-hand page. When I just tried to do this on my page, the snapping lines wouldn't show how to center that image top to bottom in my space at the top of the page, so I had to Undo (Ctrl + Z) and record the Y value for the image from the Transform panel and then move the image again and make sure that my Y value was still the same on the left-hand page.

By doing that we make sure that the chapter start images are all at the same height as you flip through the book. Also, remember to use the correct center line so that you're centered in the blue rectangular space and not to the whole page, since the margins are not even.

Finally, we need to go to the right-hand page and change the text frame there to fill the entire rectangular space. And here we are:

You may be wondering why I didn't just drag the text frames to the other page. Easy enough to do, right? Left-click drag, align to the bottom on each page, done.

The reason that doesn't work is because you have text flow already set up. It was set to flow from the left-hand page to the right-hand page, which is what we want. But if I just click and drag the two text frames to the opposite page, that reverses the text flow. It makes it so that the text flows from the right-hand page to the left-hand one. That is not what you want, obviously.

But if that ever happens you can fix it.

What you need to do is remove the text flow and then redo it in the correct direction. To remove the text flow, click on the arrow for the "starting" text frame and then click back onto that "starting" text frame.

Here I've moved those two text frames we just did to the opposite page and you can see by the directional arrow between them that the text is going to flow from the right to the left.

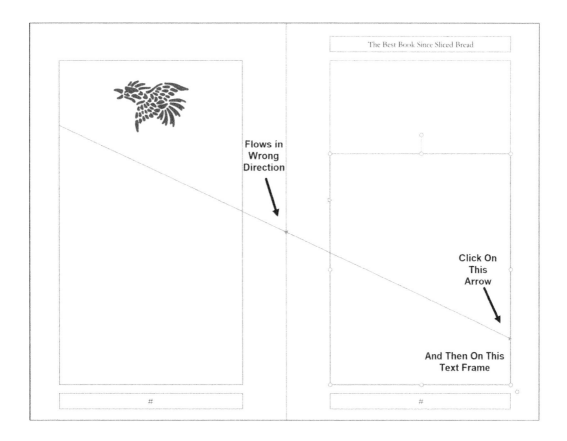

In this case you'd click on the arrow on the right-hand edge of the right-hand text frame and then click back onto that text frame. If you've done it right there should no longer be a flow line between the two text frames, and now you can create one that does go in the right direction.

But you can avoid having to do this by simply changing the heights of the text frames and leaving them in their original location.

Okay, on to the next.

TEXT AND ABOUT THE AUTHOR
MASTER PAGE

Now we're up to the end of the book. There are going to be two options that happen, depending on where your last chapter text ends. One is that it ends on the left-hand page, the other is that it ends on the right-hand page.

If it ends on the left-hand page then you'll want a Text and About the Author master page. (I've tried leaving that page blank and then putting the about the author on the next page, but it looks weird. You could do it. I think I actually had that in the last book. But ultimately it's better to just carry into something after that last page.)

If it ends on the right-hand page, I use a No Text and About the Author master page. One of the books in my stack of six here actually uses an About the Author on the left-hand side and then no more pages, but that looks really weird to me. (It's likely because in traditional publishing they have to print in groups of X pages, I think it's 8 but don't quote me on that, so they're always trying to finagle things to work with that, but for print-on-demand self-publishing, which is what most authors reading this book will do, that same issue does not exist.)

Okay. So Text and About the Author.

Duplicate the Text and Chapter Start master page. Rename. Double-click on the thumbnail. Also, for me, I'm going to left-click on that thumbnail and drag it to the end of the master page thumbnails. You'll see a blue line as you drag the thumbnail that will show where the thumbnail is going to move. Make sure that you drag it to the side of your existing master pages so that they all remain what they are and don't combine in weird ways.

To differentiate the About the Author page from the chapter headers, I'm going to move that accent image back over to the side like we had it on the title page, but keep it the same size as the chapters. At least for now. Once we have all of the text in there we may change things around.

Also, I'm going to delete the page number from the about the author side. I've seen this done both ways, but for me it's always the last page of the book even if I have back matter, so it doesn't need to be numbered and that's another subtle indication that the main story has ended.

So I click on and delete that footer.

Finally, we want to remove the text flow between the two text frames. To do that, click on the left text frame, click on the arrow on the right edge, and then click back onto the left-hand text frame.

(If you don't break that text flow, then you'll just need to remember that your about the author text is part of your main body text. I prefer to treat them separate, but it can work either way.)

Here we go:

Now let's do the other one.

NO TEXT AND ABOUT THE AUTHOR MASTER PAGE

This one will be very easy to do. Duplicate the Text and About the Author master page. Rename it. Double-click on the thumbnail. Delete everything from the left-hand page (header, footer, text frame.) Done.

BUILD THE START OF YOUR BOOK

Okay. Now that we have all the master pages we need, it's time to go back to the Pages section of the Pages panel and build our book.

The first page was already there and automatically formatted as a title page and then we added our text to it.

We also already added the Also By page. Right-click on the thumbnail for that one and choose Add Pages. We want 2 pages, After, Page 3, and the Master Page we want for this is Copyright and Chapter Start.

Make that selection and click OK.

Now right-click on that new thumbnail for Copyright and Chapter Start and choose to Add Pages again. This time choose Text and Text for the Master Page.

You should have four thumbnails that represent seven pages in your Pages section of your Pages panel:

(A quick note here. You could have added four pages that first time when you right-clicked on the Also By page and then manually changed the master page for pages 6 and 7 after they'd already been added. We'll walk through how to do that later. But for me, this is the easiest way to build the front of the book.)

Okay. Next, double-click on the thumbnail for pages 4 and 5 or scroll up to them and you'll see that we have a problem to fix:

Affinity will by default treat your document as one section, which means that it starts any page numbering on the first page and moves forward. That results in our chapter start, which should be our page 1, being numbered page 5 instead.

To fix this, click on just the right-hand side of that thumbnail in the Pages section of the Pages panel, page 5. It should have a dark blue border around just that page if you did it correctly.

Right-click and choose Start New Section from the dropdown menu:

This will bring up the Section Manager dialogue box.

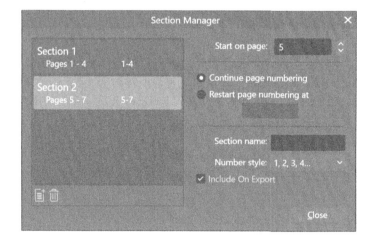

On the right-hand side of that dialogue box, change the option from Continue Page Numbering to Restart Page Numbering At by clicking on the black circle next to the restart option. The default for that should be 1, which is what we want.

Click Close and now the first chapter start will be numbered page 1. (We are using a very simple layout here, but this is also where you would go to have different numbering styles in different parts of your book or where you would assign section names if you were using those for chapter headers instead of the book title. That's covered in the next book in this series.)

One more thing we need to do here and that's flow text from page 5 to page 6 since those are different page spreads so we couldn't do that on the master pages.

In the main workspace scroll down so that the bottom of pages 4 and 5 show at the top and the top of pages 6 and 7 show at the bottom in the main workspace.

Like this:

Click on the text frame for page 5 (now numbered 1, our chapter start page). You should see the blue arrow on the right-hand edge that lets you flow text. Click on that arrow and then move your cursor to the text frame for page 6 and click on that.

Here I've clicked on the blue arrow already and it shaded the first text frame blue and now I have my cursor over the next text frame:

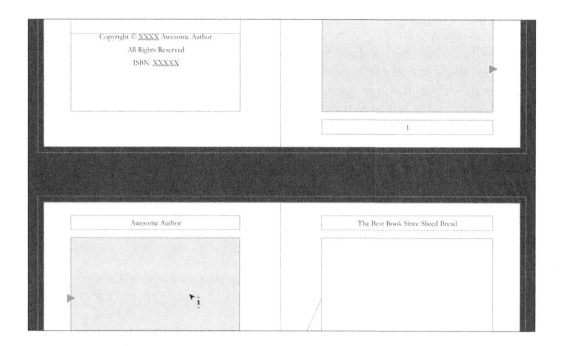

When I click on that second text frame, Affinity adds the flow line that shows that text will flow from that first master page to the next one.

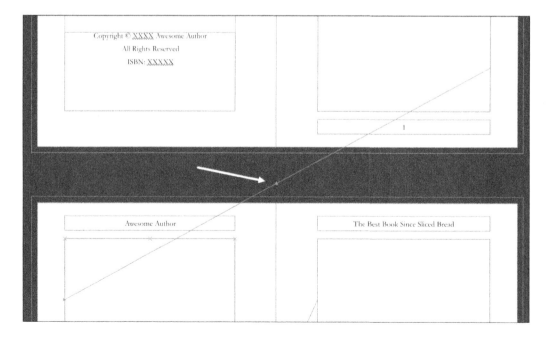

That should be the only time we have to do this. The rest will happen automatically when we add our text into the document and have Affinity add master pages for us.

Let's do that now.

ADD AND FLOW MAIN BODY TEXT

You should have the text of your book in a Word document, RTF file, or something similar. I personally do not recommend writing your book in Affinity Publisher. I think it is best used for your final formatting of your print book, but not for composition. And that's how I'm going to approach the rest of this book, with the assumption that you already wrote, edited, and finalized the text of your book elsewhere.

I personally use Microsoft Word. The only formatting I do is to use page breaks between my chapters, Heading 1 for chapter headers, and italics as needed. Everything else is formatted with the Normal style that's Word's default. But I have also used files that had text styles applied to each paragraph as well. Either one will work. But you don't have to get fancy in Word to bring that text into Affinity.

I also sometimes, if I've decided to format the ebook first, will export from Vellum as an .RTF file. That also works.

What you want from whatever source file you're using is to copy the main text of your document. Leave out any introductory text such as title, also by, etc. Also leave out any backmatter text such as an appendix, about the author, etc.

So, for example, when I export from Vellum I end up deleting the front and back matter first before I copy using Ctrl + A to select the remaining text and then Ctrl + C to copy it.

Once you have your main body text copied, go to your Affinity Publisher file. Make sure the Artistic Text Tool (the capital A) is selected. Next, click into the text frame on the first chapter page (so page 5 of the document that we've created so far) and paste the text (Ctrl +V or right-click, Paste).

If we did everything correctly up to this point, the text will automatically flow through from that page to the next two pages in your document, pages 6 and 7, which are numbered pages 2 and 3 and use your Text and Text master page:

You will then see at the very end of that last page that the blue arrow for flowing text is red. What that indicates is that there is more text that you pasted into this document than there is space to flow that text to. The text is all there, but Affinity basically hides it behind the scenes.

This is very important to understand, especially if you're someone like me who is used to working in a program like Word where if you paste 200 pages of text, you get a 200-page document.

In Affinity that text exists, even when you can't see it, unless you deliberately delete it or delete all pages it is attached to.

That little red arrow is telling us there's more text and that we need to add more pages to our document to see it.

Now, one of the beautiful, wonderful, amazing things that Affinity does is it will flow your text and add new master pages for you until all of your text is visible. It can only do this from the last page of your document, though. And it does it based upon the last master page layout you used.

That's why I had you add a Text and Text master page instead of just working from the Copyright and Chapter Start master page. Because the Text and Text master page is probably going to be your most-commonly-used master page, so might as well apply that one to all of your text now and then you only have to change your master page spread for each new chapter start.

Okay. Let's do this so you can see how it works.

Hold down the Shift key and click on that red arrow. (If you're not seeing a red arrow but a red circle instead, click on the circle first to turn it into the arrow and then Shift and click on the arrow.)

Affinity should then add as many pages to the Pages section of the Pages panel to accommodate all of the text you pasted in. I used a fairly short book for this (about 40K words), but here is my last page:

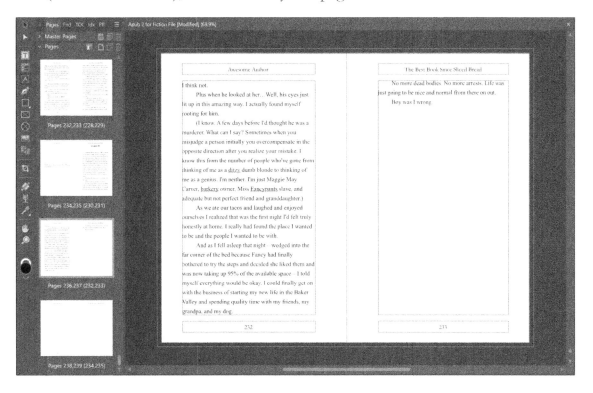

You can see that my document now has 239 pages in it. (Those last two pages are blank, likely because there was a page break at the end of the last chapter that I didn't delete.)

Affinity flowed that text and added those master pages for me in about twenty seconds, maybe less. Which is great, because I didn't have to guess how many pages I needed nor did I need to worry about flowing text between the pages I added. Affinity did all of that for me.

Which means all I have to do now for the main body is format my text, assign a different master page format to those pages where I have a chapter start, and then address issues like widows, orphans, and italics.

Once I've done all that I'll end with my About the Author page.

TEXT STYLES

Up to this point we have manually formatted our text. We haven't had a lot of it, so that was pretty easy to do and I didn't want to bog us down in a discussion of text styles so early on. But for the main body of your document, text styles are essential because they will save you a tremendous amount of time.

Think of a text style as a shortcut that has a font, font size, font style, and other attributes already stored. When you apply that style to your text, it applies all of those attributes to your text for you so that you don't have to go and choose the font, font size, etc. over and over again.

This means your formatting is more consistent, because you don't format one paragraph one way and the next a slightly different way.

It also saves a lot of time to use a text style. You can apply it with a click of a button or a Ctrl shortcut rather than have to hunt down all of the various settings.

For a basic novel or short story collection, you will have four potential text styles to create for the main body text:

1. Chapter Title

2. First Paragraph

3. Main Body Paragraph

4. Separator

In some of my non-fiction I have more than that because I have subheaders or sub-subheaders or numbered lists or bulleted lists, etc. But for a basic title, that should be it.

Let's create each of those now. I'm going to go back to the start of chapter 1 because three of the four occur on that first page.

CHAPTER TITLE

In general, your chapter title should be in a larger font size than the main body text. Often it will be in a different font as well. This is where a sans-serif or decorative font can be used for a special appearance.

I tend to name my chapters Chapter 1, Chapter 2, etc. but most of the books sitting here on my desk just use 1, 2, 3, etc. when that's the way the chapters are named. For me, keeping the word chapter in there lets me apply my chapter title format more easily, so I'm going to leave it.

But let me make sure real quick that I don't use the word chapter anywhere else. To do that, I'm going to go to the Find and Replace panel, type "chapter" into the Find field and then click on Find.

Here are the results:

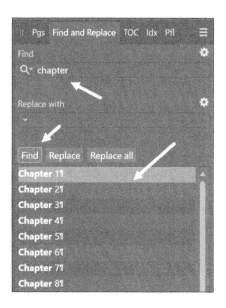

The entire list of results are all chapter names. I have no entries where it says something like, "this is the worst chapter of my life." Good.

Now let's come up with a format to use for those chapter headers. I'm going to increase my font size to 30 and choose a font I have called Fountain Rough. It's a script font with a texture to it so you'd never use it for the main body text in a novel, but it can work on a book cover or, in this case, at the top of chapters.

I'm not madly in love with it, but we'll keep it for now.

I also need to go to the Paragraph panel on the top right, because right now there is a very large space between the chapter title and the first paragraph. This is because of how the text was formatted when I brought it in from my RTF file:

The value I want to change is that 48 on the right-hand side in the second row that's for the Space After Paragraph. It's fine to have it be more than the font size we're going to use (which will probably be 10 or 12 pt), but 48 is just a bit too much there. I think I want 24. As you enter different values, you'll see the text adjust:

Okay. That's better. All of our chapters in this book will be one line only so I don't need to worry about that Leading value, but if I had chapter names (like I do in non-fiction) that were going to wrap to the next line I'd want to probably change that value as well.

(You can update a style later if needed, so we're not locked into this, but it's best to finalize your styles before you start walking through the document page-by-page and applying master pages and fixing widows, orphans, etc.)

Now that we have our format for the chapter title, let's turn it into a text style. To do that, select the text and go to the Paragraph Style dropdown menu in the dynamic menu up top:

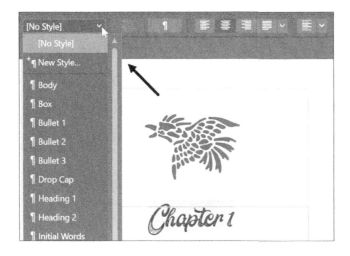

It is the second style dropdown menu, not the first.
(You could also use the Text Styles panel, but that's never the way I do it.)
Choose New Style. That will open the Create Paragraph Style dialogue box:

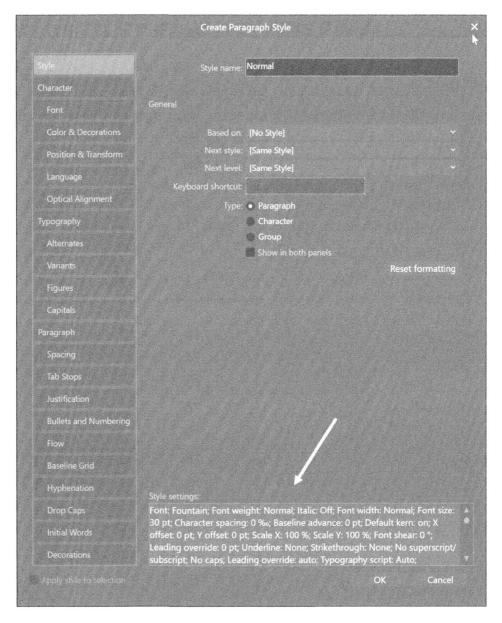

At the bottom of the dialogue box is a description of everything that Affinity thinks creates that style. You can see the font type listed there, that it's not italic, that it's 30 pt, etc. Don't worry too much about that for this one, but it'll be useful to know about that in a moment.

In the Style Name field, type a name for your style. Mine is going to be Chapter Title

Also, click into the Keyboard Shortcut field. What makes using styles speed things up is having shortcuts assigned to each one so that you can just use that shortcut to apply the style.

For me, and this is not necessarily the best way to do this, I use Shift + 1, 2, 3, 4, etc. for my text style shortcut keys. It gets me in trouble at times if I find that I need to edit text in my document and that I need to use an exclamation point, at sign, pound sign, etc. Because I try to use a pound sign and instead change my paragraph formatting.

But since I use Affinity Publisher primarily for formatting and not writing or editing, those are the keyboard shortcuts I use because the keys are very easy to reach and keeping them in order (1 for chapter title, 2 for first paragraph, 3 for main body paragraph, 4 for separator, etc.) makes them easy for me to remember.

Choose what works for you. But whatever you choose, click into that box and use the shortcut. Affinity will then populate that box with the shortcut you used like it did here with Shift + 1 for my Chapter Title style:

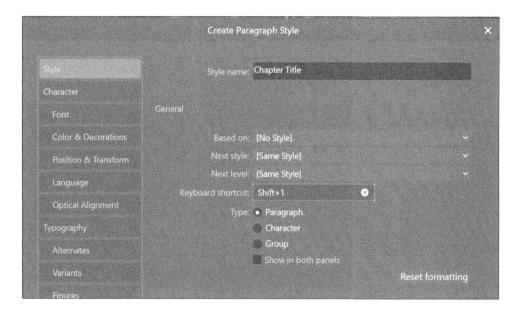

Click OK and now you have that style to use.

FIRST PARAGRAPH

Next let's create our first paragraph style. This is the style to use at the start of each chapter or the start of each section.

I'm now down to five sample novels on my desk. All five have a first paragraph of the chapter that is not indented. Three of the five also don't indent the first paragraph after a break, two do.

I should also note that four of the five that I just looked at use a drop cap for the first letter of the first paragraph in the chapter, but we're not going to get that fancy here.

Okay.

I'm going to use Garamond for the font. No paragraph indent. 12 pt. Regular. Justify Left. And use hyphenation as well. (Five of five in my little sample stack here use justify left, four of the five use hyphenation.)

Another option for paragraph formatting would be left-aligned which leaves a ragged margin on the right-hand side. That's what I do for large print, along with no hyphenation, because it ensures that all words are equally spaced and that someone doesn't have to struggle to follow the word to the next line.

And, actually, often in my regular print books I will do justified left and no hyphenation and just fix weird gaps with a little tracking adjustment because I seem to have something against hyphenation, but that's not the norm.

(Sometimes, because I am a creature of chaos at heart, I'll just use hyphenation on one little line or paragraph where I used a really long word and there's no good way to fix it without using hyphenation. Don't be me.)

Okay. So. Let's make these changes to the first paragraph of the document. Select the text. Font and font size happen in the dynamic menu up top.

Next, we can go to the Paragraph panel. I'm going to make the Leading 14 here. That's the space between the lines. I'm also going to make the space after the paragraph 0. Hyphenation is in a section lower down in that panel. We just need to check auto-hyphenation. I also expand Baseline Grid and make sure Align To Baseline Grid is turned off.

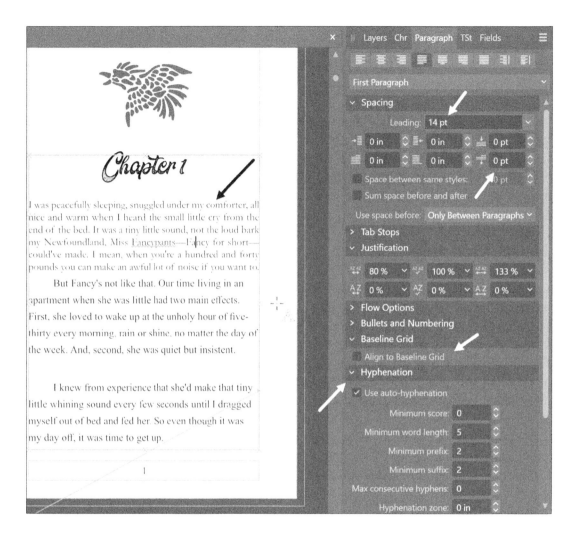

You can also expand the Flow Options section and have Affinity prevent orphans and widows for you, which is what I do for large print. But for regular print books I prefer to do that manually, because sometimes I can tweak the spacing in an earlier paragraph on a page to bring a line up and eliminate the orphan or widow that way, which ensures that my text starts and ends at the same point on facing pages.

(We'll cover that more in the chapter on fixing widows and orphans.)

Great. Done. Now let's add that as a new style. I'm going to use the shortcut Shift + 2 for this one.

MAIN BODY PARAGRAPH

The main body paragraph style is really easy to create, because it's just the First Paragraph style with an indent added to it.

So I'm going to click on that second paragraph there and use Shift + 2 to apply my first paragraph style to it and then change the indent for the first line to .2. Here it is:

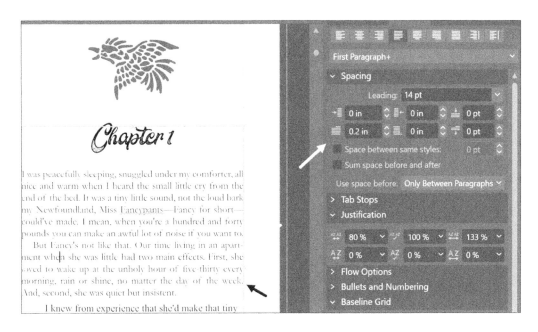

Once more, we can go to the paragraph style dropdown menu to create a new style here, but before we do that, I want to show you something:

Note how that says First Paragraph+ for the paragraph style name. This is how Affinity indicates that you took a paragraph style, First Paragraph, and modified it. So it's telling me that the paragraph of text that I'm currently clicked into is not actually formatted using that style. It started with that style, but I changed it.

Which we know, because we did so deliberately. But if I had done so because I wanted to change the First Paragraph formatting, then I'd need to do one more thing to update that particular style to incorporate my changes. And that is to click on the Update Paragraph Style option to the right of the dropdown. If I click on that option, Affinity will update my First Paragraph style to reflect my changes.

So, for example, just a moment ago, you didn't see this, but I initially had a 14 pt value for the space after my paragraph. But I realized I needed that to be zero. So I changed the value to zero and then just clicked on Update Paragraph Style to incorporate that into my existing style I'd just created.

Okay. Here, though, we want to create a new style so we click on the dropdown arrow to make that New Style choice.

That gives me this Create Paragraph Style dialogue box which I've filled in with my style name and shortcut:

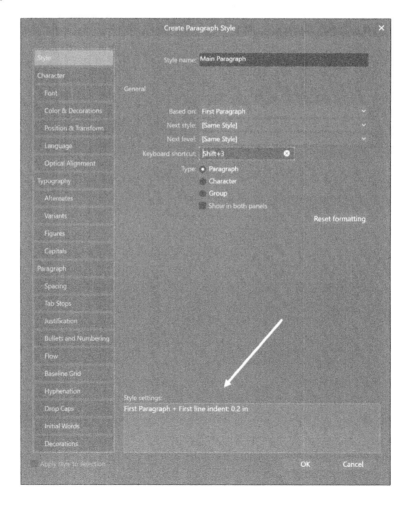

Look at the bottom there where it says Style Settings. Instead of the long paragraph listing all of the possible settings that we saw for First Paragraph, this one just says "First Paragraph + First line indent: .2 in."

Basically what that is saying is that my Main Paragraph style is the First Paragraph style with a change to the first line indent. Any change I make to the First Paragraph style will also apply to this style, except for any change made to the paragraph indent.

So let's say I decided I wanted to use Baskerville URW for my font. I only have to make that change to the First Paragraph style.

Or let's say I decide I want to use a 10 pt font instead of 12 pt. Same thing, I only need to change the First Paragraph style.

My chapter title style, however, remains completely separate.

What I usually end up with is one style grouping for my accent elements and another grouping for my main text elements. So I format one style in each group and then apply that style to any other text in my document that should be part of that group and edit from there. That way I can easily modify the entire group by going to the "base" style, in this case First Paragraph for my main text elements.

We sort of cheated here and I didn't make you use text styles for the front matter of this book so that text is not tied into the main text right now, but we'll clean that up in the next chapter.

For now, let's save this as a new style, Main Paragraph, with a shortcut of Shift + 3.

Next, let's create a style for our paragraph separators.

SEPARATOR STYLE

Here is a page where I have a couple of separated sections within a chapter:

As I write I just use * * * to create these separations. Sometimes I leave it that way in the final version. In my cozy mysteries I change the font over to Ennobled Pet so that they're little paw prints. A non-fiction book I'm reading right now uses a little image of books on a shelf. Some books use a blank line (although be careful there because you'll probably need to use something if that break falls at the top or bottom of a page).

If you do use an image, it takes more effort to position the image correctly. I prefer to use a font that has embellishments as part of the font to get that effect, because then Affinity treats that like text and centers it for me automatically. Fonts like Wingdings come with a lot of shapes that you can use.

For this one, let's use the Ennobled Pet font to get our result. (It's a free font you can download.) First, though, I want to apply my paragraph formatting to the paragraphs before and after the section break so I can see what it will look like. So Shift + 3 for the paragraph above, Shift + 2 for the paragraph after.

Since this is going to be a different font and font size, I'm just setting it up standalone. If it were more tied into the settings I used for First Paragraph I could apply that style first and then work from there like I did for the Main Paragraph style.

Here it is with the Ennobled Pet font, 14 pt, with 0 pt above and 8 pt below:

I think that works, but I want to test it on the other separator on this page to see if that top spacing is only working because the last line of the paragraph is short.

I could create a new style for this right now and then use my shortcut to apply the style to that other separator, but let me take this opportunity to show you the Style Picker tool that is available in Affinity Publisher 2.0 but was not available in the original program.

The Style Picker Tool lets you take the style on a selection and apply it to another one. I think you can do this with any object, but so far I've just used it for text.

The Style Picker Tool can be found in the secondary menu for the Color Picker Tool. So click the little white arrow next to the Color Picker Tool and then click on Style Picker Tool:

Your cursor will look like an eyedropper. When the eyedropper is angled towards the right, that's when you can select a style:

As soon as you select the style you want to copy by clicking on that text, the eyedropper will angle in the other direction.

You can then select the text or object you want to apply that style to. Use the Esc key to switch it back to copy mode if needed. The style will apply one character at a time with text, so be sure to select all of your text.

That's how I just applied the format I created here to the second set of separators on this page:

> take him home. Now."
>
> I sneezed. Crazy cat lady and her frickin' white-haired ball of allergies. If that cat was around for much longer I was going to need a shower or have to risk my throat swelling shut.
>
> ❀ ❀ ❀
>
> Now, before we continue, I feel I need to say a few things because you may be a cat lover and I don't want you to get the wrong idea here. I have nothing against cat lovers in general. I think anyone who can love any animal, be it a dog, cat, or rhinoceros, is a good person.
>
> And as a crazy dog lady myself I understand how someone can love their cat to the point of dressing it in costumes and talking to it in a baby voice. Only reason I don't do that with Fancy is she'd probably sit on me the first time I tried to put her in some weird outfit.
>
> So I have nothing against cat people. Or cats for that matter. (Other than the fact that I am insanely allergic to them and that, somehow psychically knowing this, they all try to rub up against my legs or sit on my face. True story: I once woke up to find my friend's kitten curled in a little ball on my throat.)
>
> So when I call her a crazy cat lady it has nothing to do with any other cat owner on this planet. I just wanted Janice Fletcher and her sneeze-inducing feline friend to leave.
>
> ❀ ❀ ❀
>
> "This isn't fair." Janice glared at me as Patsy crowded up

I think I still like that spacing, so let me turn that into a new paragraph style with the shortcut of Shift + 4. Done.

* * *

Now we can go do a little quick clean-up to tie our front matter text and headers and footers into the First Paragraph text style. You don't have to do this next part, I'm just going to show you, because it will make changing your document font later much easier to do.

FRONT MATTER TEXT STYLE CLEAN-UP

In order to create a template where all of my text is nestled under the First Paragraph style, I'm going to go back now and quickly fix my front matter and master pages. If you don't care about this, you don't have to do it. Just keep in mind that you'll need to manually adjust those front matter sections if you ever change your main body font.

First step, go to the Pages panel and expand the Master Pages section. We're just going to work our way down through the thumbnails in that section.

On the Also By page I've decided to switch that over to use Garamond so that it matches the rest of the book. To do that, I select the header text, apply the First Paragraph text style (Shift + 2) and then bold, Align Center, change the font size to 16 pt, and add an 8 pt space after.

Save that as Also By Header text style.

Next, select the book titles, Shift + 2 to apply the First Paragraph text style, Align Center, use a 6 pt space after.

Save that as Also By Titles text style.

Move on to the copyright and chapter start page. Select the copyright text. Shift + 2. Align Center. 6 pt space after each line. Save as Copyright text style.

Finally, go to the footer that has the pound sign. Select it. Shift + 2 to apply the First Paragraph text style. Align Center. Center Vertically. Save as Header and Footer text style with a shortcut of Shift + 5.

Go through the rest of the master pages and apply the Header and Footer style to the headers and footers using Shift + 5. (This is admittedly one of those times when having just one-page master pages would save time, but it still only took me about two minutes to do.)

And done.

Now if I ever decide that I want to change the font used throughout my document, I can do so by just changing the First Paragraph text style.

And, actually, any attribute I didn't specifically change for one of the other styles that I change for the First Paragraph text style will apply to those styles as well.

Just do watch out if you change font size, such as for large print, because you will have to manually adjust any of the dependent text styles that had a font size specified, such as the Also By Header text style.

* * *

If you ever want to see which text styles are the main text styles that others are based off of, go to the Text Styles panel and use the three bars at the end of the panel tab listing to change the view to Show Hierarchal. (The default view is to show them alphabetically.)

That will collapse the styles down to the primary style and then you can expand a style to see the ones that are based on that style. Like here where you can see that I've expanded First Paragraph and there are five styles indented and listed underneath it:

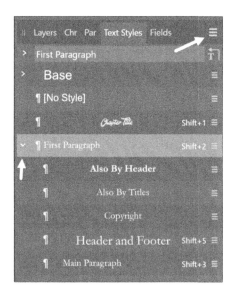

* * *

Okay. Now let's go apply styles to our main body text.

APPLY STYLES

Since the large majority of the text in the main body of a document is going to be the Main Paragraph text style, that's the first style I assign to all of my text in the main body of my document.

So I click into the text frame for the start of Chapter 1, use Ctrl + A to select all of the main body text, and then use Shift + 3 to apply my Main Paragraph text style to all of it.

I get something like this on that first page:

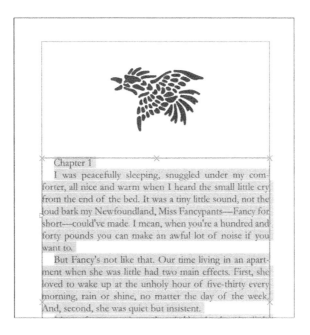

Now all I have to do is go through and apply chapter title, first paragraph, and separator formatting when it's needed.

Depending on how you named your chapters or how you format your separators, there may be a few shortcuts you can use for this.

CHAPTER TITLES

Because my chapter titles are all Chapter [X] and I didn't use the word chapter anywhere else in the book, I can use the Find and Replace panel to format my chapter headers.

To do this, I go to the Find and Replace panel and type "chapter" in the Find field.

Next, I click on the little gear widget next to Replace With and use the Paragraph Style secondary dropdown menu to choose Chapter Title.

Finally, I click on Find and then on Replace All.

You can click through on a couple of entries to see that each chapter header now has that style applied to the text:

Note that it didn't just apply to the word "chapter", but also applied to the number. That's because this is a paragraph style and it applies to the entire "paragraph" even when that paragraph is just one line.

Separators

I can do something similar with my separators since I only use * * * for that purpose. (At least in that book.)

This time I look for * * * and replace with the Separator paragraph style.

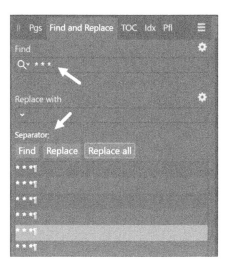

FIRST PARAGRAPHS

I like to remove the indent from the first paragraph after a separator, which means I need to apply my First Paragraph text style to those paragraphs.

I can use the search results for my separators to locate each one by clicking on each search result for * * * in the Find and Replace panel. Then I can click into the main document on the paragraph below each separator and apply that First Paragraph text style.

It's easier to do it this way than to walk through the document so I don't miss one, which can be easy to do.

After that, if I wanted, I could search again for "chapter" and do the same for the first paragraph of each of my chapters. Although that one I usually apply as I walk through the document and apply my master pages. Either way works.

DOUBLE-CHECK TIME

The next big step is going to be walking through the entire document and making any little tweaks for widows, orphans, weird spacing, etc. while also applying our master pages for each chapter.

But before we do that it's time to take a moment and see if everything looks okay.

Do you like the amount of space between your chapter headers and the first line of text? Do you like the spacing between paragraphs? Between lines? Do you like the spacing around your separators? Do you like the placement of any image you used? What about your headers and footers?

Anything else that needs fixed now? Because if you decide later that you don't like it, you'll have to do a lot of duplicate work. So this is the moment to get any of that fixed if you want it fixed.

The reason to figure this all out now is because the spacing of elements and text on the page will impact where your chapters end, which will impact which master page to apply.

Also, the spacing impacts whether you have widows or orphans that you need to deal with. If I have an 8 pt space between my chapter title and my first line of text, that will create different widows or orphans than if I have a 16 pt space.

So work all of that out now. Make sure your elements are what you want them to be before you move forward.

During this process I noticed an issue with my Text and Text master page:

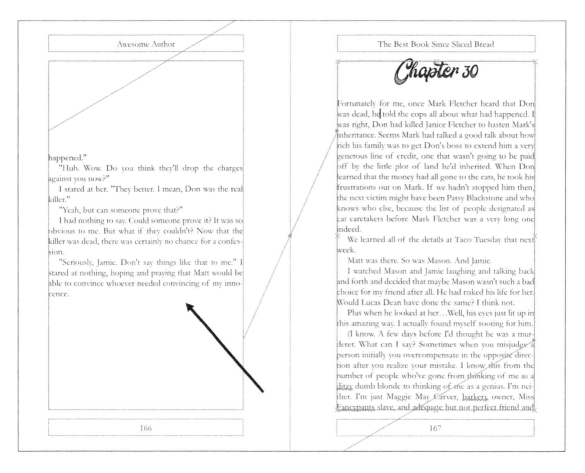

The text in that left text frame is set to center vertically. We don't want that. All of the text frames for text need to be set to Top Align. So I went back through my Master Pages section of my Pages panel and checked my text frames to make sure they all use Top Align instead of Center Vertically.

That's something that really only shows itself when there's text in the text frame and it's not enough to fill it. This particular issue doesn't impact where lines fall on the page, but it's still good to fix it as soon as you notice it.

Okay, so double-check. Make sure everything looks "good". Fix it if you need to. And then we can continue.

WIDOWS, ORPHANS, AND OTHER ISSUES

Widows and orphans are single lines alone at either the top or bottom of the page. Here you can see examples of one of each:

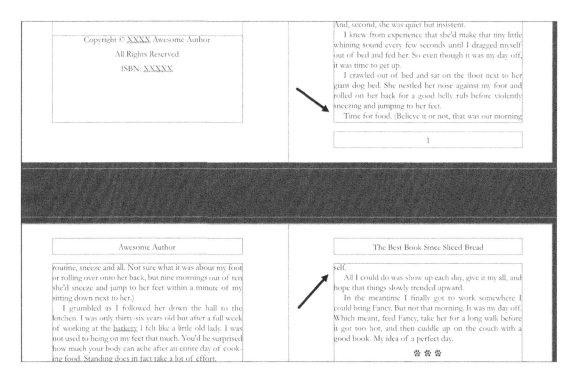

Ideally, you try to avoid having either one. But sometimes, you just can't. Like here, that top one where there's a single line at the bottom of the page, I have no good options for fixing that. I could force that line to the next page if I wanted, but I really don't, so I'm just going to leave it.

But I absolutely do not like that "self" at the top of page 3. Especially because it's part of a hyphenated word.

The way I try to fix widows and orphans is I try to identify a paragraph earlier on that page or the prior page where I can pull text up one line.

Especially when I'm not using hyphenation this is often possible because justifying text can put extra space between words to make the text reach the end of the line.

Here's what I have to choose from:

The best candidate on this one is actually the last paragraph that's falling over to the next page. So I'm going to select that text, go to the Character panel, and click on the dropdown for Tracking:

I hold my mouse over each of those negative values starting with -5% and stopping around -20%. Beyond that the text starts to look too cramped.

In this case, -5% brought the rest of that line back up to the prior page:

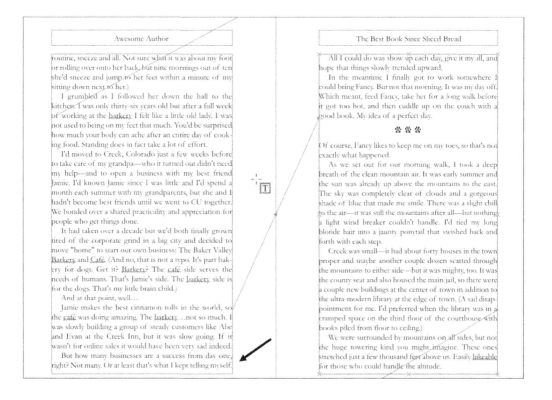

You really can't see any difference between that paragraph and the ones around it and now we don't have that little "self" carrying through to the next page.

Great. I'll continue through the document looking for lines like that that can be fixed. You have to do this from first chapter to last, because the changes you make to adjust one widow, orphan, or other line issue will impact all other lines in that chapter.

Other things to watch for are paragraphs that end with one really short word alone on a line. I believe the guidance is three letters or less. So if a line ends with just the word "too" you want to try to pull that up to the prior line.

If you use hyphenation, watch out for any scenario where too many words are hyphenated in a row. I think that's called pig bristles. Affinity lets you tell it the maximum number of consecutive hyphens. The default looks to be zero. But you could still have a scenario with say three out of five lines in a paragraph hyphenated that wouldn't look good on the page.

Try not to have a chapter end with just one line on the final page. Two lines on the last page you can maybe get away with. Three or more is better.

Also pay attention to any situation where the same word is on three lines in a row at the same spot. (Rare, but I think I've seen it once.)

And, if you're not using hyphenation but are justifying your paragraphs, look out for unseemly white space on the page where words have been spaced out too much on a line.

This is one of those times where reading a lot in print is a benefit because things will be jarring when they look wrong.

Now let's talk about the other adjustment you need to make at the same time, and that's applying your master pages for chapter starts.

APPLYING MASTER PAGES

The way we had Affinity flow our text through the entire document was by letting it use the Text and Text master page throughout. But that's not the master page you want to have for your chapter starts. So each time you reach a new chapter, you need to apply a different master page.

This requires you to make a decision. Do you want your chapter starts to fall where they may, on the left or right as the case may be? Or do you always want your chapters to start on the right-hand page? You need to make that decision now.

Because, here, is our first chapter that we need to change:

Depending on what you decide, it's either going to look like this:

Or like this:

You can see that the decision you make has a profound impact on where your text falls, especially across three hundred pages or more of text.

So make that decision now. We are going to use the "let it fall where it may approach" for this novel. So we need to apply the Chapter Start and Text master page to this two-page spread.

To do that, go to the Pages section of the Pages panel and locate the thumbnail for these pages:

The advantage to applying your chapter title style first is that it makes it easier to see in the thumbnail so you can easily locate those pages. But even if you don't have that, you should know your page numbers, and you can see below each thumbnail the page numbers in the overall document as well as the page numbering for that section in parens.

So here we were looking for pages 8 and 9 and we can see that it's shown as "Pages 12, 13 (8,9)". Click on that thumbnail.

Be sure that you have chosen both pages in the thumbnail, not just one of the two. The whole thumbnail should be surrounded by a blue box.

Right-click and choose Apply Master from the dropdown menu.

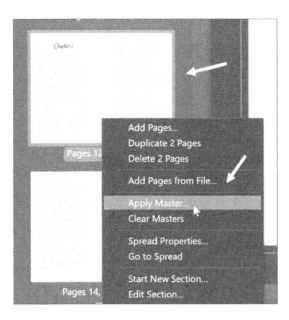

The Apply Master dialogue box will appear:

Use the dropdown at the top to choose the master page you want. They'll be listed in the order you have them in the Master Pages section of the Pages panel.
  Click OK.

That two-page spread will now use the master page you chose and the text will reflow appropriately.

Move forward from there dealing with widows, orphans, etc. and applying your master pages for each chapter until you reach the end of the document.

ITALICS AND BOLDED TEXT

The great thing about using text styles is that you can format most of your text in less than five seconds. The bad thing about using text styles is that when you do that you lose any italics or bolding or other special formatting that you used for individual words in that text.

I save this step for the end because I don't use italics that much. If you have whole paragraphs of text in italics, you may want to include this step with your walkthrough of the document to apply styles and master pages because italics do take up a different amount of space than plain text, so can shift your text slightly. Usually when it's one or a handful of words, it's not a big issue. But if you have whole paragraphs in italics, do that formatting as you walk through the document.

What I do, though, is wait until the end and then use the search function to locate the text I need to italicize. You'll need to search in your source document for any italics and then locate that same text in Affinity and apply italics to it.

In Word, use Ctrl + H to open the Find and Replace dialogue box, go to the Find tab, and then click into the Find What box, and use Ctrl + I. It should look like this:

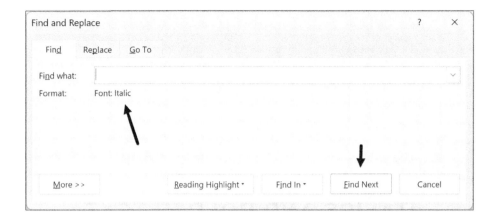

Click on Find Next to find the next text in the document that has italics applied.

For each word that is in italics, then go to the Find and Replace panel in Affinity and type into the Find field the word or a phrase that includes the word that will make it easy to find. Click on the Find option.

You should see a listing of results that match:

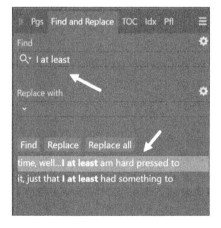

Click on the one you want.

Affinity will take you to that page in the document and highlight the text you searched for. If the search term was the text that needed to be italicized, you can just click on the slanted I in the dynamic menu or use Ctrl + I to apply italics to that search result.

Otherwise, click into the document, select the text you want to italicize, and then apply italics to it.

It used to be that the search function didn't work with apostrophes so you couldn't search for "I'd call" or something like that, but I just tested it and it looks like that issue is now fixed.

When you're done, in Word you need to return your search function to its regular state. So click into the Find What box and use Ctrl + I two more times to return it to a search that doesn't require the text to be italicized before you close the dialogue box.

Repeat for bolded text or any other uniquely formatted text that you need to adjust for.

As I mentioned above, italics do take up a little less space than regular text, so be sure to check when you add italics or bolding to text in a paragraph that it doesn't shift things around.

If it does, I either visually check to make sure it didn't create any new orphans or widows or I use Tracking to expand things just enough to put the lines back to what they were.

TIDYING UP

After you've formatted all of your text and applied your master pages, chances are at the end you'll run into one of two issues.

The first issue, and for me the more common outcome when formatting novels, is that when Affinity first flowed your text for you it flowed it to more pages than you actually need. My paragraph formatting takes up less space than the RTF or Word document formatting that I bring in.

So I get to the last page of text and I have something that looks like this in the Pages section of the Pages panel:

There are a lot of blank pages there that I don't need. To delete blank pages, select them by clicking on the first one, holding down shift, and clicking on the last one.

And then right-click and choose Delete [X] Pages from the dropdown menu where X is the number of selected pages:

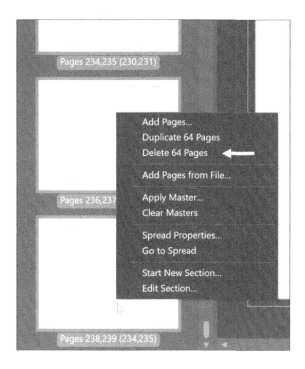

That will delete all of those pages for you.

With non-fiction, I usually have the opposite problem because I use a lot of images and when I insert those images that pushes my text down the page until ultimately I get to the end and have something that looks like this:

It's a little hard to see, but there is a red circle along the right edge of the text frames. It's going to be on the edge of every text frame in the document when this happens. What that is saying is that there is more text than can be fit into the available text frames.

The solution is to simply reflow your text once more. So click on that little circle on the last page in your document to turn it into an arrow, and then Shift and click on the arrow to flow your text.

Now, one thing to be careful about with this is that if you have a lot of text hidden back there, you want to make sure to change that last page's master page to the Text and Text master page first. (Or whatever your most common master page layout is.) Otherwise Affinity will flow to whatever the current master page layout is for those last two pages, in this case a Text and Chapter Start master page.

I deliberately created this scenario so only had one page for it to flow to, so it doesn't really matter. But I sometimes have thirty pages to flow and then it does.

Ctrl + Z, Undo, is your friend if you mess that up. Just undo, change the last page layout, and then try again.

You can also select that range of pages that Affinity added and then right-click and choose to Apply Master to all of them if you accidentally use the wrong master page layout. Problem is, that likely won't be the same number of pages required and you'll have to then delete pages or reflow again.

ABOUT THE AUTHOR PAGE

Okay. Assuming you've finished with the main body of your document, there's just one more master page to add (for our simplified layout), the About the Author page.

In this current example, my novel ends on the left-hand page, so I just need to change that last thumbnail's master page to Text and About the Author:

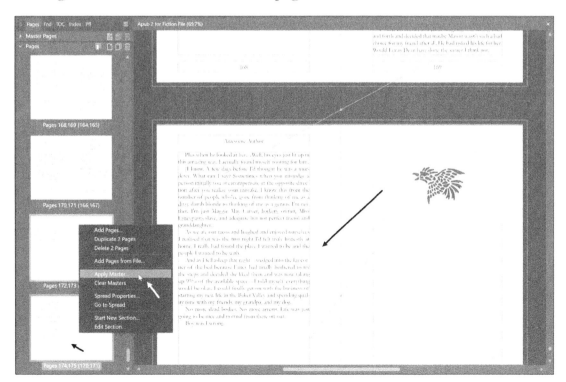

For some reason, in my case, when I did this the text flowed to the about the author page and not the last page on the left-hand side of the spread. If that happens to you, just fix the flow. (Click on the arrow from the right-hand edge of the text frame on the prior page and click back on that text frame to break the incorrect flow, and then click on the arrow on the right-hand edge of that text frame and click on the left-hand page text frame on the final spread to flow to the correct page.)

(I don't know what will go wrong for you, but expect that something will, which is why I leave these little mentions in here.)

Once that final page spread is working properly, simply click into the text frame on the about the author page and add whatever you want to say about the author.

I just had another glitch here where it insisted on using my accent font even when I applied my text styles to the text. So I had to manually format the text using Garamond. I don't know what caused that. I eventually did get it back to the text style I wanted to use.

Sometimes, things are just glitchy and you have to work around them. Sometimes that's user error (me in this case), sometimes it's a computer issue, and sometimes it's going to be the program you're working in. I usually just find a way around unless it's a fatal issue in which case I go digging for a better solution.

Okay.

Here is our final spread:

The novel ends on the left-hand page and then the right-hand page is our about the author.

The other outcome you may have at the end of your book is that the text ends on the right-hand page. In that case, you need to add two more pages, so left-click on the final thumbnail, and Add Pages.

You want 2, after the last spread, and the master page should be No Text and About the Author. Click into that right-hand text frame, add your text, and format as needed.

Since we didn't link the about the author text frames to the rest of the document, they are standalone and you can type your text directly into them without worrying about it ending up in the main body of your document.

If that does ever happen where the about the author is part of the rest of the document, you can force your text into that frame by using a frame or page break.

I'll talk about that in the next section because you might need it for other things as well.

OTHER COMMENTS, TIPS, AND TRICKS

FRAME OR PAGE BREAK

There will be times when you want to force text to the next text frame. I do this often with non-fiction but it could come up with fiction as well. To insert a frame break, click where you want the break to happen, then go to Insert→Breaks→Frame Break.

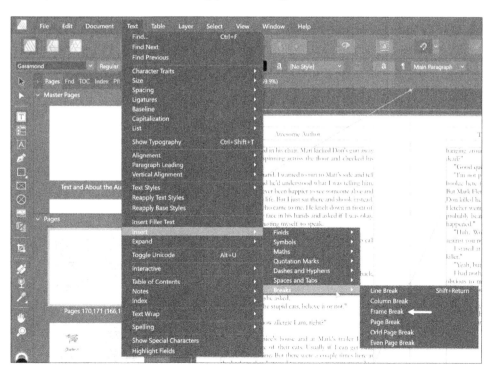

I believe for the setup we used here a Page Break would also work.

One thing to note is that it always inserts an extra line when it does this, so you'll have a blank line and then the rest of the text from the prior frame and will need to delete that blank line. (I don't know why it does that, but it does.)

OTHER FRONT AND BACK MATTER ELEMENTS

In the next book we'll get more complicated about additional front and back matter elements, but I think you can see how to create more master pages if you need them and then add or break text flow between pages as needed. But I just wanted to acknowledge that this is a very basic layout without a lot of bells and whistles. For example, my YA fantasy books include a character guide and terminology guide in the back, and most of my non-fiction have an index and a table of contents.

SPELLCHECK

You may have noticed that Affinity has added red squiggly lines under certain text in my document. That's an indication that it thinks I have spelling errors. I use in the cozies the term "barkery" to refer to a bakery for dogs, for example, so it's flagged each of those uses.

If you go to the Preflight panel, you can see all of the identified issues:

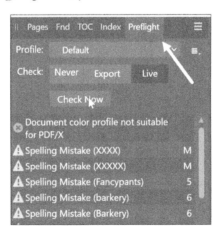

It doesn't just list spelling errors, but for me that's most of it for a novel. You can double-click on any of those entries to go to that page.

Right-click on the entry in your document to see spelling suggestions or to tell Affinity to ignore the error or learn the word.

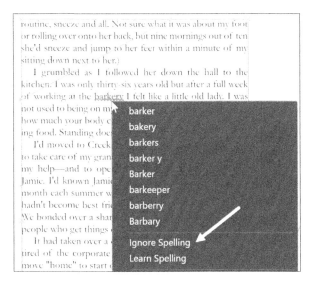

I have a high tolerance for clutter, so I usually don't do anything and just scan the list to make sure my editing passes didn't miss an error. Although I do believe that before it wasn't quite so obvious in the document itself.

PREFLIGHT

In addition to spelling errors, the Preflight panel will identify a number of issues for you. I use it to see when my index or table of contents need updated (a more advanced topic) or when my images are not proportional anymore as well as if I've failed to meet the minimum DPI for print.

If you don't want Preflight to identify a type of error or you do need it to identify something, click on the Preflight panel and then click on the three lines at the end of the tabs listing and choose to Edit Profile. This will bring up the Edit Preflight Profile dialogue box where you can choose what type of warning level something is assigned.

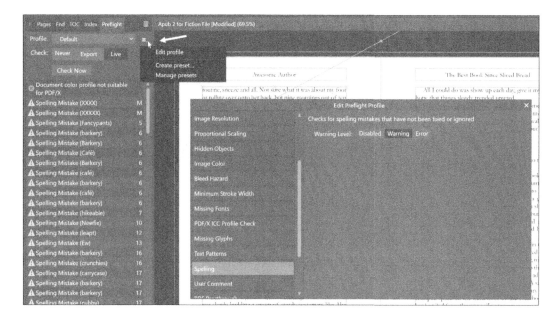

You can also customize some parameters. For example, by default it will alert if your image resolution is below 72 DPI, but I set it to 300 for print.

Also, in Affinity Publisher 2.0 Affinity now tells me that the document color profile is not suitable for a PDF/X file when I have it set to greyscale. You can submit a file to Amazon KDP or IngramSpark that is in color and still have them print it in black and white. But it means that they do the converting on their end.

So if that error bugs you, use a CMYK profile instead of greyscale. So far, I've just ignored it and the books I printed with Amazon and Ingram turned out just fine. But if you're concerned, definitely be sure to order a proof copy to review.

If you have any alerts in preflight, Affinity will warn you about them and ask if you want to look at them before you can export your file, so it's always a good idea to look through it before you attempt to export.

CHANGE IMAGE

This is more something for covers or ads, but you can swap out an image in Affinity. The option that is always available is to go to Window in the top menu and then choose Resource Manager. This will open the Resource Manager dialogue box which will show all of your images in your document.

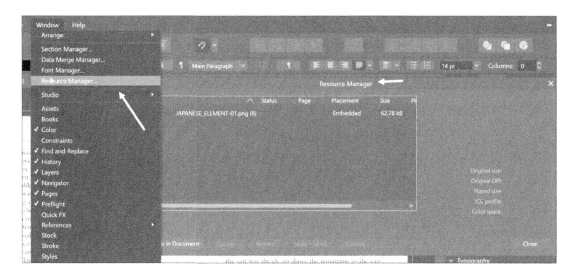

Click on the one you want to replace and then click on the Replace option at the bottom and navigate to the new image you want to use.

Another option is available if you click on the Move Tool and then click on the image on the master page where you inserted it. A Replace Image option will show in the dynamic menu up top.

Any adjustments you made to the prior image after it was inserted into the document will also apply to its replacement. (Rotation is the one that usually catches me out with that.)

OPEN RECENT FILE

I've assumed throughout this that you know the basics of opening and closing Affinity, etc. But do know that under File→Open Recent, you will see a listing of all of your recent Affinity files so that you don't have to go open the file wherever you have it saved. This is pretty standard, but just wanted to mention it.

ZOOM

Zoom can be found under the View menu. You can also use Ctrl + = to Zoom In and Ctrl + - to Zoom Out. I usually find I don't need zoom for print layouts, but just in case. Zoom to Width, Alt + Shift + 0, is also a useful one.

SCROLL BARS

There are scroll bars below the main workspace and on the right-hand side that will let you scroll through your document.

I also often use the wheel on my mouse to do so. Just make sure the cursor is over the main workspace or the thumbnails in the Pages section first, whichever you want to scroll through. (I often start trying to use my mouse to scroll and am on the wrong one.)

EXPORT AS PDF

Okay. Check back through your document one more time to see if it's ready to review. If it is, time to export to a PDF.

Go to File and click on Export. You will likely get this message:

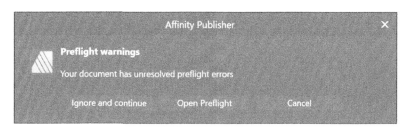

Since I already looked at Preflight, I click on Ignore and Continue. If you choose Open Preflight that will cancel your export.

Next you'll see the Export Settings dialogue box:

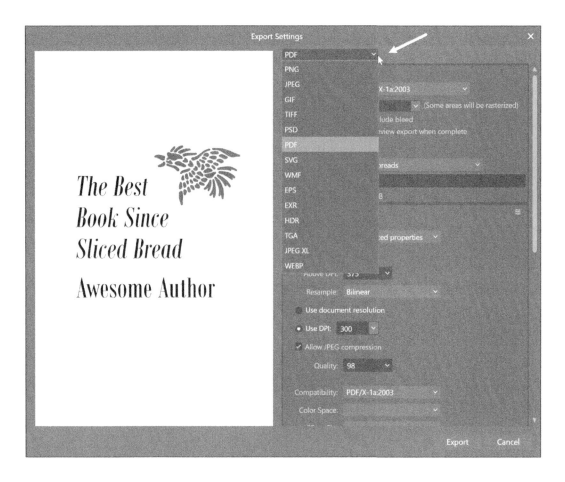

There is a dropdown at the top where you can choose the format to export to. For a print book published through KDP or IngramSpark, you want PDF.

(I use PNG and JPEG for cover or advertising images.)

For a simple novel without a lot of images in it, use the Preset dropdown to choose PDF/X-1a:2003 or PDF/X-3:2003. The IngramSpark file creation guide asks for PDF/X-1a:2001 or PDF/X-3:2002, but those aren't available choices. I've never had an issue submitting with X-1a:2003.

(Note here, I am not a graphic design professional. If this really matters to you, I am not the authority to trust on this.)

I always check the box to preview the export when complete.

This next bit is very, very, very important. Under Area it is going to default to All Spreads.

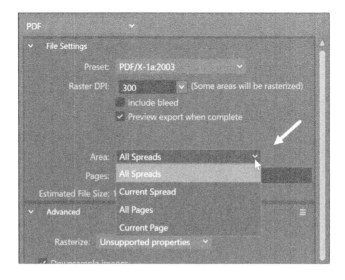

For reviewing the file, that's fine. It's almost better because it lets you see the pages in the appropriate location, left- or right-hand of the page.

But when you are ready to submit to Amazon KDP or to IngramSpark, you must change this setting. It needs to be set to *All Pages*. The PDF you submit should have as many pages as your final book does.

Our example I've been working with has 175 pages showing in the Pages section of the Pages panel. That's what I need to see in my PDF, too. If I see 87 or something like that, I have a problem and will need to re-export.

Another way to check that you exported as All Pages is to look and see if the default view in your PDF viewer shows one page at a time. If you export as All Spreads, the first page will be standalone, but the rest will be paired.

For the final file be absolutely sure that you use All Pages not All Spreads.

You don't need to worry about the Advanced settings for a basic title like this. Just choose that preset for PDF/X-1a:2003, change the dropdown to All Pages, click on Export, and tell Affinity where to save the file.

FINAL DOCUMENT CHECK

I always do one final, thorough document check on the PDF file.
Look for the following:

1. Spelling errors in the title page
2. Overlap of text and images in the front matter
3. Missing ISBN (this is why I use XXX in the master page, so I'll notice it)
4. Correct copyright year
5. All chapter starts have the correct master page applied
6. Page 1 of Chapter 1 starts with the page number 1
7. Headers and Footers are correctly spelled and what they should be
8. No header or footer on a page without text
9. No unsightly gaps in text, widows, orphans, really short words ending a paragraph, single lines on a page, etc.
10. All chapter titles have been properly formatted
11. All separators have been properly formatted
12. All first paragraphs have been properly formatted
13. No random blank pages anywhere
14. No header at the top of a chapter start page
15. Headers and footers are at the same height on the left- and right-hand pages.

16. Text is italicized or bolded as needed

17. Images in the document are clear not blurry (if blurry the image may be missing and you may need to link to it again through the Resource Manager or the DPI may not be high enough)

Basically, does it look right? Sometimes this is best seen by printing the document. I worry less about it with novels than with non-fiction titles that have a lot of images, but you should always scroll through at least once. This is also why I always publish to Amazon KDP first when I publish a print book, so I can use their previewer for one final flip through the book.

If you find issues, fix them in Affinity, and then re-export and re-review. Rinse and repeat until the book is ready to go. Once the file is ready, then with both Amazon KDP and IngramSpark you just upload the PDF file along with a cover PDF file and they do the rest.

REUSE AN OLD BOOK

I promised you earlier in this book that you weren't going to have to go through this whole lengthy process every single time you create a book. And that's because once you have one book created, it's pretty easy to delete out the content from that book and reuse the file for a new one.

So let's walk through how to do that now, because there are a few important things to keep in mind if you're going to do this.

Step one, open the old book file and save it as a new document.

Now, go to the Pages section of the Pages panel and find pages 8 and 9. If you added more front matter at some point, it won't be pages 8 and 9 but instead whichever pages represent the third page spread in the main body of your document.

What you want is to keep the beginning of your book and a Text and Text master page to use to flow your text, but the rest of it can go. So click on that third page spread in the main body of your document, hold down Shift, go to the last page spread in your document (the also by for us), click on it, right-click, and Delete [X] Pages.

In my case that was 168 pages.

The next step is to click into the text frame of the main body of your document, use Ctrl + A to select all of the text in the main body (including the 160+ pages of hidden text, because it's still there even if the pages aren't), and Delete. If there were any images in picture frames on those first three pages, delete those, too.

And if your final page spread is not a Text and Text master page, change that over.

Also, go to your Fields panel and update the book title or author name, if needed.

You should now have a seven page (or longer) document that's ready to start editing for the new book you want to create. Go to the title page and update it with your new book information. Make sure the Also By is still accurate or update it in the master pages section. Change the year and ISBN number for the copyright notice. And then dump in the new text of your new title and walk through the process starting with Add and Flow Main Body Text.

Easy enough. You'll already have the master pages we created here as well as the text styles, so it's just a matter of applying them or updating the primary text styles as needed.

CONCLUSION

Okay, there you have it. How to format a basic book that uses a simple accent image using Affinity Publisher 2.0.

Now, a reminder that I am self-taught and am not perfect. So this works for me and has let me format a large number of print books. But if you think I'm wrong or there's a better way to do that or you'd never put the copyright notice on the page I did, that's fair.

Every single time I write a non-fiction book, even one I've written before like this one, I start from scratch because I in the interim have learned new things or may have decided to approach the problem from a different angle. We don't often realize it but we are always learning and growing, so what you and I know today is nothing compared to what we'll know next year.

At the end of the day, if it works, it works, right? I am a firm believer that there is no "only one way to do things" in this world. There's just "did it get you a satisfactory result"? If it did, then great. If not, then you find a new answer.

What we walked through in this book, does that for me and will hopefully do that for you.

Also, if it's too complicated or messy to format your books or you find you don't enjoy it, don't be afraid to switch to a tool like Vellum or Atticus or use D2D's option instead. We each only get so many hours in a day and while a nicely-formatted book does help, the difference between formatted in Affinity and formatted by Vellum probably isn't worth stress and headache if that's what formatting does to you.

Anyway. I hope that won't be the case now that you've read this book. If there's something that was confusing or you get stuck, reach out at mlhumphreywriter@gmail.com.

And if you want to keep going and explore tables of contents, indexes, and inserting images into the body of your document, then continue on to Affinity Publisher 2.0 for Book Formatting Part 2.

Affinity Publisher 2.0 For Book Formatting Part 2

CONTENTS

INTRODUCTION

This book is a continuation of *Affinity Publisher 2.0 for Book Formatting Part 1* which covered how to create a basic black and white print title using master pages, text styles, and a simple accent image. That book also covered how to flow text and export to PDF along with other beginner-level topics.

This book will assume that you already know all of that material and build from there by covering more advanced print-formatting topics, including how to insert a single table of contents, multiple tables of contents, and an index. We'll also cover how to use chapter names instead of the book title in headers or footers, how to have multiple columns of text on a page, how to merge multiple book files into one, and how to insert images into the body of your document.

It is the equivalent of *Affinity Publisher for Non-Fiction*, which was written for the original Affinity Publisher.

If you bought Affinity in late 2022 or later then you probably have version 2.0 and this is the right book for you, but it's best to double-check. You can tell when you open Affinity which version you have because the launch screen for version 2.0 will say Affinity Publisher 2, like in the screenshot below:

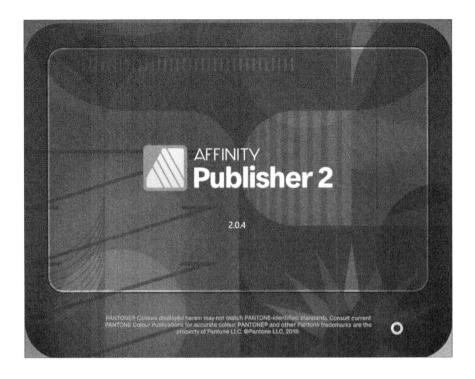

At this point I have formatted over a hundred books in Affinity, but most of those were in the original version of the program, so what I'm doing here is saying, "I know how to do this in the original Affinity program, how does that now work in Affinity Publisher 2.0". Which means that I may not catch all of the new bells and whistles.

But my approach does work and when you finish reading this book you will have a way to do all of the topics listed. I can't promise it's the absolute, most efficient way, but it does work and it works well enough I haven't felt the need to track down a better solution.

Okay. So.

Let's dive in and start with the easiest topic: how to use chapter names instead of the book title for the header or footer. (Again, I'm going to assume you know what was covered in Part I so already have formatted master pages to work with.)

CHAPTER OR SECTION NAMES FOR HEADERS OR FOOTERS

In Part 1 we set up master pages that used the book title in the header. The Text and Text master page looked like this:

As mentioned in that book, that title that you see in the top right header in that screenshot is actually the Title field and the text you're seeing there is what we entered for Title in the Fields panel.

But if you want to use chapter or section names instead, then that works a little differently. So first step if you're working from an existing file like we are here, is to delete the existing field from that text frame.

Go to the master page, click on the Artistic Text Tool, click on the text frame that contains the title, Ctrl + A to select the text, delete.

(If you weren't working from an existing file, then create a place for your text to appear like the text frame we have here for the header.)

The next step is to click into the text frame if you haven't already, go to the Text menu option, go down to Insert, then Fields, and then Section Name.

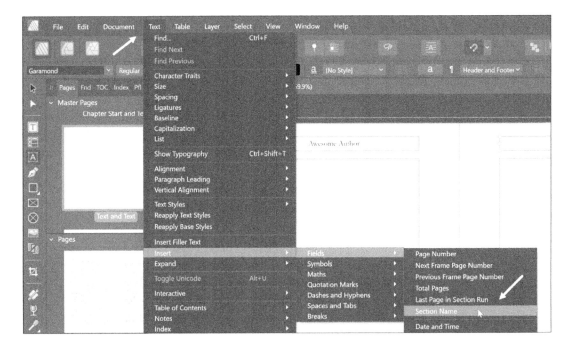

And there you have it:

Note that it inserts the field name <Section Name>, because it's going to be different throughout your book depending on the section. (I wish they did the same for the Author and Title fields, but they don't. At least not as of April 2023.)

If you're adapting an existing file, make this change for all of your master pages that use the Title field. For me that's Text and Text and Chapter Start and Text.

Updating the master pages or formatting them to incorporate the Section Name field is step one. Next, you need to give Affinity section names to use. If you were using just the book title before, you're probably going to have a Section Manager that looks like this:

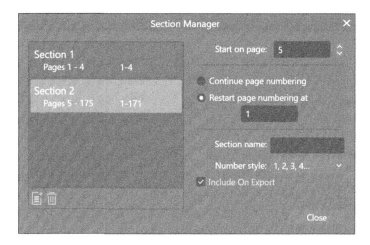

There are only two sections in the document, one for the front matter, one for the main body and backmatter. And the only reason you have two is because you want the start of the first chapter to be numbered page 1.

Note that neither section has a name. The Section Name field is blank and none is listed in the left-hand section listing.

Here, in contrast, is the Section Manager for one of my non-fiction titles:

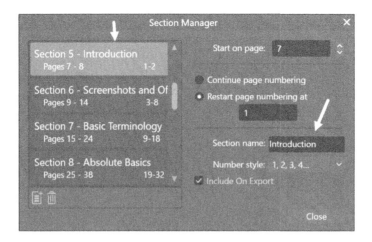

Note that for the selected section, the Section Name field on the right-hand side is now populated (with the text "Introduction") and that a section name is listed for all of the sections in the section listing on the left-hand side of the dialogue box. For example, "Section 5 – Introduction" and "Section 7 – Basic Terminology".

That Section Name field has to be populated for Affinity to use section names.

For each section you will manually input the value, so it does not have to match the chapter name, which is helpful when a chapter name is too long.

It's also helpful for when you want to have a header that spans multiple chapters. For example, when I create an omnibus of my fiction titles, so three of them in one book, I have a section for each novel. The text I use in my header is the title of the novel not the individual chapter names.

Let's go create some sections now to see how this works.

In the Pages section of the Pages panel, find the start point of the first chapter or section that you want to create. Select only the one page of the two-page spread that is the start of the chapter or section. Right-click and choose Start New Section from the dropdown menu.

(If you already created a section that starts on that page, choose Edit Section instead.)

This will open the Section Manager dialogue box. Enter a value for section name and hit Enter. While you have this open, also confirm that the page numbering choice is correct. In general, you're not going to restart your page numbering after the front matter so the "continue page numbering" option should be checked and also the number style will likely be 1, 2, 3, 4.

Click Close.

You'll then need to walk through your document and right-click on the first page of each of your chapters or sections or wherever you want to create a new header, and choose to Start New Section for each one to add it into the Section Manager.

You *can* add a section directly in the Section Manager using the small page with a plus sign icon at the bottom of the section listing, but I don't recommend it. It assigns the page number for the section in a weird way in my opinion. But try it if you want.

You can also edit more than one section at a time with the Section Manager open. Just click onto the section you want to edit on the left-hand side to bring up that section's information and then make your edits. (I sometimes need to do this when I have multiple documents I've merged and need to fix the page numbering settings.)

Every single page in your document must be assigned to a section. Which means that a section will contain all pages from that section forward to the next section you designate. The place to be especially aware of this is at the end of your document. There's the possibility (because I've done it) that you create a section for your last chapter and then forget to create another one for any backmatter and your backmatter ends up using the last chapter's name in the header.

To edit a section name later, just right-click on the thumbnail (or really any thumbnail) in the Pages section of the Pages panel, choose Edit Section, and then go to that section in the Section Manager and change the value for section name.

If you ever need to delete a section you created, that can also be done in the Section Manager by clicking on the section on the left-hand side and then using the trash can below the section listing.

And here we go, a page header that uses section name, in this case for page 3 of Chapter 1 in my document:

To summarize. If you want to use chapter or section names in your document header or footer there are two steps involved. First, make sure your master page is set to use the section field name. Second, create sections and assign them a name.

SINGLE TABLE OF CONTENTS

For simplicity's sake right now, I am going to keep working with the file we created in the prior book in this series, which was a fiction title that used chapter names like Chapter 1, Chapter 2, etc. even though a table of contents is not standard for a novel like that.

Tables of contents are common for short story collections and for non-fiction. I have also seen them used in novels when there are named chapters. And I have used them in novels that included backmatter I wanted a reader to know about, such as a character listing, terminology, or summary of a prior book.

Since I'm using the file from before, the first thing I need is a master page that will work for my table of contents. I copied my Also By master page and edited it to get this:

I made the accent image smaller and moved it to the corner and also moved where the text frame starts higher on the page. For the first page of a table of contents I choose not to include a page number. I named this master page Table of Contents.

Next step is to insert that master page into the document. I'm going to put mine after my also by page, so I go to the Pages section of the Pages panel, right-click on my page spread that includes my also by text, choose to Add Pages, and select 2, After, and Table of Contents for the master page in the Add Pages dialogue box.

Once the new pages are added to my document, I double-click on the thumbnail for those pages, click into the text frame on the right-hand page in my main workspace, and move my cursor to the line below the text that's already there, Table of Contents.

Now we're ready to insert the actual table of contents.

To do that, go to the Table of Contents panel, which we placed in the top left corner in the last book. (If you don't have it, go to Window→References→Table of Contents and that should open it for you.)

This is the top of the panel:

Click on the Insert icon in the top left corner which looks like three pieces of paper stacked on top of one another.

If you used text styles like we did in the last book, chances are this is what you'll get:

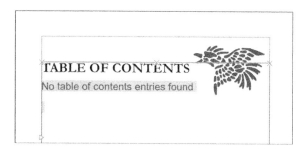

That is because by default Affinity is going to use Heading 1 and Heading 2 text styles to drive the table of contents entries. You can see that in the bottom of the Table of Contents panel where those two boxes are checked:

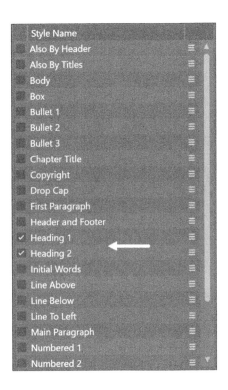

Uncheck those boxes and check the box for the text style or styles that you used to create your chapter or section headers. In my case, that is going to be Chapter Title. As soon as I did that, the table of contents turned into this:

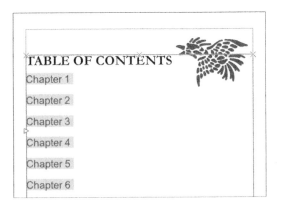

Better. But I also want page numbering. To include page numbers, go back to the Style Name section of the Table of Contents panel and click on the three lines at the end of the row for each style you want to use. In the dialogue box that appears, check the box for Include Page Number:

Now I have this:

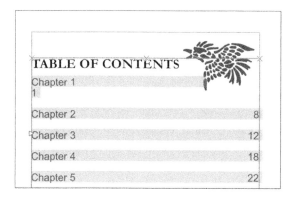

You can see I have page numbers now, but I also have an issue because my image that I included on the page dips down enough to make the page number for the first chapter wrap to the next line. I need to go back to the master page and do one of two things. I can either move the start of the text frame down a bit so that doesn't happen, or I can change the Text Wrap Settings related to that image so that any text that overlaps the image jumps the image. (I could also just delete the image and then center the header.)

In this case, I'm just going to change where the text starts.

But I have another issue. The default text formatting for table of contents entries uses Arial 12 point and the rest of my document is using Garamond.

If you click on a text entry in the table of contents, you'll see that Affinity assigns a text style to TOC entries. In this case it's calling the style TOC 1: Chapter Title since this is the first table of contents in the document and the text style that's feeding into these entries is the Chapter Title.

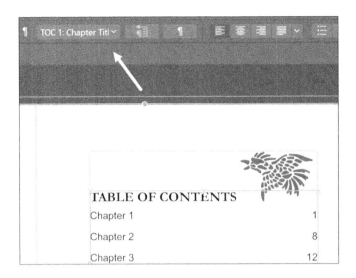

Each text style that feeds into your table of contents will have its own assigned text style. So if you use two different text styles to populate your table of contents and want to reformat the entries, you'll need to do this twice.

Take one of the entries in the table of contents and change the formatting to what you want to use, in my case Garamond 12 pt. I will often also, for non-fiction, use the Typography section of the Character panel to make my entries small caps or all caps as well.

Click on Update Paragraph Style to apply that change to the text style. (As a reminder the update option is in the dynamic menu up top and to the right of the dropdown that shows the text style name.)

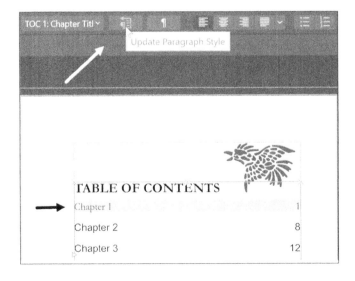

That should automatically update all of your TOC entries that use that style. But this one is sometimes finicky.

For example, for me just now it didn't update all of my entries. It updated the page numbering, but not the text side of the entry. And even when I just highlighted the text for a chapter entry and did it again, it still failed to work. But unchecking and rechecking the box for Chapter Title in the Table of Contents panel fixed it. Of course, I then had to tell it to use page numbers again because it reverted back to the original settings.

So if something doesn't work immediately, play around with it a bit. It may be the program not you.

It is possible to just manually format your text in your table of contents. You could select all of the text in the table, format it to your heart's content, and do it that way. But the problem is, that you can never ever again update that table of contents. Because as soon as you refresh the table, Affinity will go back to the assigned text style for those entries which is in Arial 12 point.

This is also why you should never fix a typo or anything like that directly in the table of contents. Go find the entry in the document that has the typo and fix it there. Everything you see in your table of contents is auto-generated and populated by Affinity and so can be overwritten. Which means, ideally, you insert that table of contents and never touch anything in it after it's inserted.

(With the exception of changing the formatting and then saving that as the TOC formatting, of course.)

Let's say you did have a typo. Here we are, I just looked at this list and Chapter is misspelled for Chapter 1:

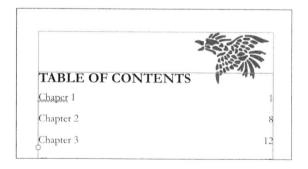

The way to fix this is to go to Chapter 1 and change it there. Next, go to the Table of Contents panel, click on the text frame that contains the table of contents so that you can see the options for it, and click on either Update or Update All Table of Contents at the top of the panel:

In this case, both options will do the same thing and update this table of contents.

You can also, go to Preflight and click on the Fix button next to "One or more tables of contents entries need updating":

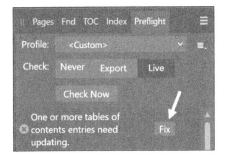

If you ever manually update your table of contents, Preflight is going to tell you that your table of contents entries need updating. So be very careful if that's how you choose to handle an issue. It can be easy to forget, click on Fix in Preflight, and then break whatever it was that you manually changed.

If you have a lot of table of contents entries, like I do here, they will require more than one page and you will see that the text frame is overflowing. In that case, you will need to create and insert another master page to handle that and then manually flow the text from this page to that one.

Let's do that in the next chapter as part of showing you how to have two types of page numbering in a document.

USE TWO TYPES OF PAGE NUMBERING

The front matter in a book, which is everything that falls before the main text of the book is supposed to use a different page numbering than the main book. The front matter uses small Roman numerals (i, ii, iii, iv, etc.) whereas the main part of the book uses the more traditional 1, 2, 3, etc. Backmatter, if numbered, usually continues with the main body numbering.

Now, it turns out that the way I have handled page numbering for front matter in the past is wrong. When I include it, I just start the numbering with my table of contents so that page two or three of my table of contents is numbered ii or iii.

But, I just took a gander at a bunch of books on my shelf and when they number the pages they treat the entire front matter as the same. So that the second or third page of a table of contents ends up being page x or page viii or wherever it happens to fall in those first pages, even if none of the other pages in the front matter are numbered.

Good news is that if you keep your table of contents short you can avoid this headache altogether because none of the books I checked used a page number if the table of contents fit on the first page. Many also didn't use page numbering if the table of contents was only two pages long.

But let's say you do want to number that second page in the table of contents. Or maybe you have an Introduction to a classic novel that you want to treat as front matter and it needs to be numbered differently.

Easy enough to do.

First, make sure that your master pages are set up to display page numbering for that part of the book. If it was the table of contents, you'd have the first page not show a page number, but any subsequent pages show it, for example.

Second, go to the Pages section of the Pages panel and right-click on one of the thumbnails to choose Edit Section and bring up the Section Manager:

Chances are Section 1 will be your front matter. Use the Number Style dropdown for that section to change the numbering style to lower-case Roman numerals:

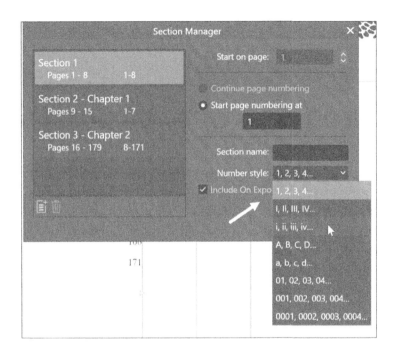

That will ensure that any of the pages in your front matter that use a page number in their layout include the appropriate value.

Your next section should already be set up, but if it isn't make sure it uses the 1, 2, 3, 4, etc. numbering style and is set to restart at 1.

And here we go:

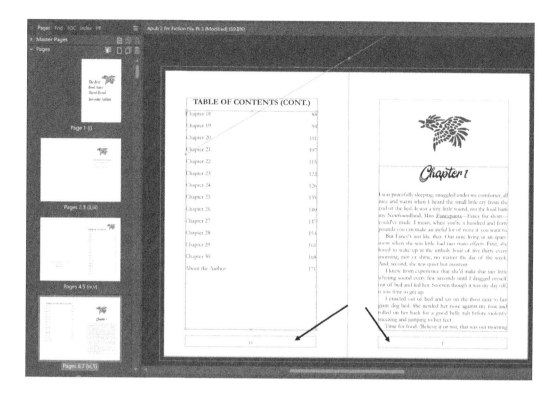

I moved the copyright notice around since I have a table of contents now, which means my front matter ends with the last page of my table of contents. You can see here that that last page of my front matter is page vi and then the main text starts on the next page with page 1.

Personally, even though I know it's wrong, I still prefer to just number my table of contents pages and not all of my front matter. If you want to do that, then you need to create a new section for the table of contents and tell Affinity to restart numbering for that section in addition to setting the number style to lower-case Roman numerals. However, keep in mind that you shouldn't do that if you have more than one element in your front matter that needs to be numbered.

COLUMNS

We'll circle back to tables of contents again later and discuss how to have more than one in your document, but first I want to cover a couple other topics, namely indexes and how to have multiple columns of text on the page.

When I insert an index into the back of my non-fiction books I use two columns per page, because a short entry like that doesn't need its own dedicated line. Here for example is the first page of the index from one of my Word 365 books:

You can see that using two columns works just fine for an index like this. So let's go set up a master page for this and I'll show you how to have multiple columns on a page.

I'm just going to copy the master page for Text and Text and then convert the right-hand page to an index page. So, go to the Master Pages section of the Pages panel, right-click on the Text and Text thumbnail, Duplicate, rename, drag to the end, double-click on the thumbnail.

I want page numbering, so we can leave that, but I'm going to shorten the text frame in the main text area and drag down what is now a header and turn it into an Index label at the top of that space using my Chapter Title Header text style to replace the text currently in that field.

I also removed the text flow between the two text frames. Here we are:

Click on the Move Tool if you don't already have it selected (the black arrow) and then click on the main text frame on the index page.

On the far right of the dynamic menu up top there should be a Columns option. If it isn't visible, it's because of how big your screen is or how much you have your screen zoomed in. Click on the double-arrow at the end of the row to see the columns option.

Here, for me, for example, the gutter width setting for columns is not immediately visible:

You can also open the Text Frame panel, which is under Window→Text→Text Frame. The second section of that panel is for Columns settings and the third is for Column Rules. I've minimized General here and expanded those two sections so you can see the available options:

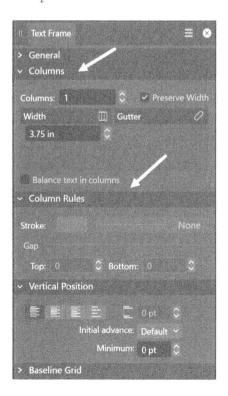

When you choose to have multiple columns, Affinity will by default preserve the width of the text frame and will apply a .333 inch gutter between them.

Here, for example, I have a text frame that is 3.75 inches wide. Choosing two columns creates columns that are each 1.708 inches wide:

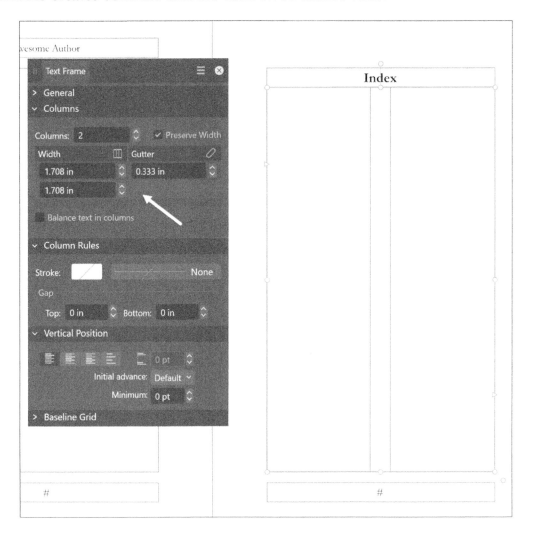

If I ask for three columns, it defaults to 1.028 inches for each column with .333 inch gutters between them:

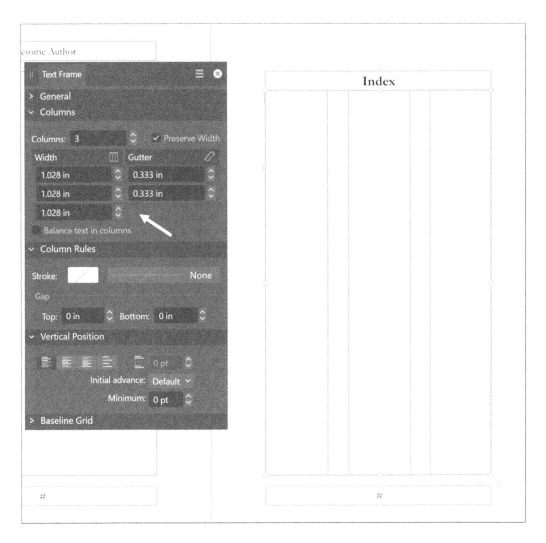

You can edit those values and Affinity will adjust. Here, for example, I changed one of the gutters to .125 inches and it changed my column widths to 1.167 inches and the other gutter value to .125 inches:

Keep in mind that the blue lines you see right now in that text frame will not exist on the printed page. So it will just be text in three columns with that space between them.

It is possible to add a line in the gutter between your columns. That's in the Column Rules section of the Text Frame panel.

Click on the white box next to Stroke. It will say Column Rule Stroke Fill if you hold your mouse over it:

When you click on that box a pop-up dialogue box will appear that lets you choose the color of the line that you're going to place between the columns. It looks like it defaults to the Color tab, but for what we're doing here which is black and white, we can click over to the Swatches tab and choose the black swatch:

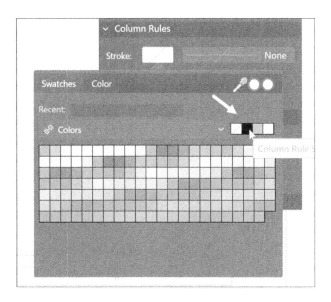

By default Affinity will use a line that is .2 pt wide:

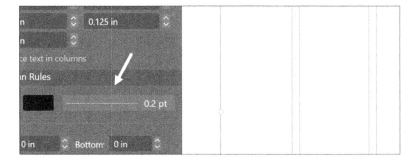

Click on the line in the Text Frame panel to bring up a pop-up dialogue box that allows you to specify the line width and style. By default it is a solid line, but you can also have a dotted line by clicking on the dotted line image in the style row. To change the line thickness either click into the field and type a value or click and drag the white button along the Width line:

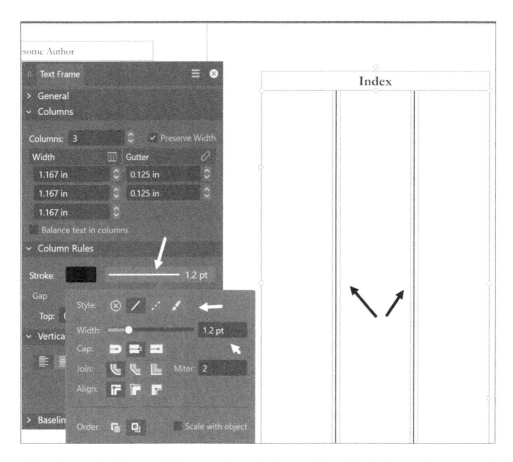

Above I've kept the line solid but made it 1.2 pt wide which is much more obvious.

If you want the lines to have a shape, like an arrow, at the ends, that is under Start and End. Here is the dropdown menu that shows all those available choices:

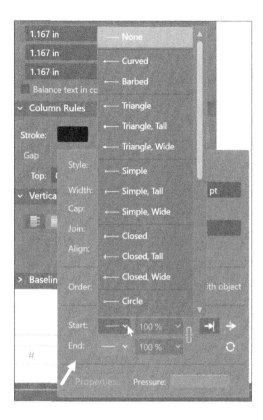

You can also set the line so that it doesn't start at the very top or end at the very bottom by changing the Top and Bottom values in the Column Rules section of the Text Frame panel. Here I've set the lines to start half an inch below the top of the frame and to end a half an inch above the bottom of the frame:

I should also note here before we drop in text that it is possible to have uneven columns by changing the Width values in the Columns section of the Text Frame panel, but I wouldn't recommend it because the text is going to flow from one column straight to the next. If you're looking for uneven columns, chances are what you're trying to do is probably more of a two-column text frame next to a standalone narrow text frame that contains pull-out quotes or something like that.

But it is possible to do. Affinity will auto-adjust the width of the next column to keep the total text frame width the same unless you uncheck that "preserve width" box.

Okay. Text time. I'm going to go back to two columns for this.

But first I'm going to remove that line between the columns. To do that, click on the rectangle next to Stroke in the Column Rules section of the Text Frame panel and click on the "no color" option which is a white circle with a red line across it.

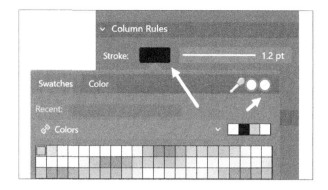

I want to add my text in the actual document, not the master page, so I need to go to the Pages section, add pages, add this master page style, and then I can drop in some text.

I want to ultimately use this for an index, but there's something else I want to show you with columns that is best seen with regular text, so I have dropped in part of the last chapter of a book here so you can see the text flow:

Index

Fortunately for me, once Mark Fletcher heard that Don was dead, he told the cops all about what had happened. I was right, Don had killed Janice Fletcher to hasten Mark's inheritance. Seems Mark had talked a good talk about how rich his family was to get Don's boss to extend him a very generous line of credit, one that wasn't going to be paid off by the little plot of land he'd inherited. When Don learned that the money had all gone to the cats, he took his frustrations out on Mark. If we hadn't stopped him then, the next victim might have been Patsy Blackstone and who knows who else, because the list of people designated as cat caretakers before Mark Fletcher was a very long one indeed.

We learned all of the details at Taco Tuesday that next week.

Matt was there. So was Mason. And Jamie.

I watched Mason and Jamie laughing and talking back and forth and decided that maybe Mason wasn't such a bad choice for my friend after all. He had risked his life for her. Would Lucas Dean have done the same? I think not.

By default, the text is going to completely fill the first column and then move on to the top of the next column as you can see above. If you want the text to be evenly balanced between the two columns, you need to check the Balance Text In Columns field in the Columns section of the Text Frame panel. That will give the text this type of appearance instead:

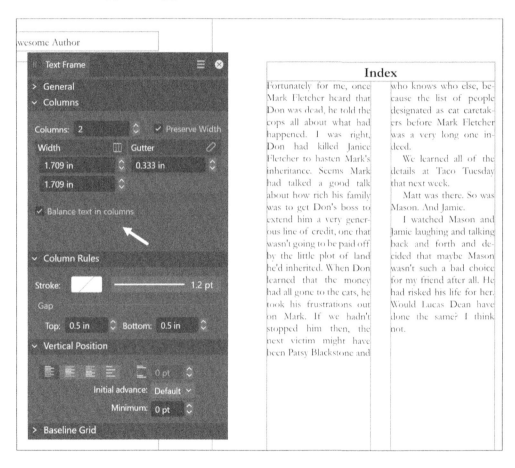

It is also possible to force text into the next column using a Column Break. Click where you want to break the text and then go to Text→Insert→Breaks→Column Break:

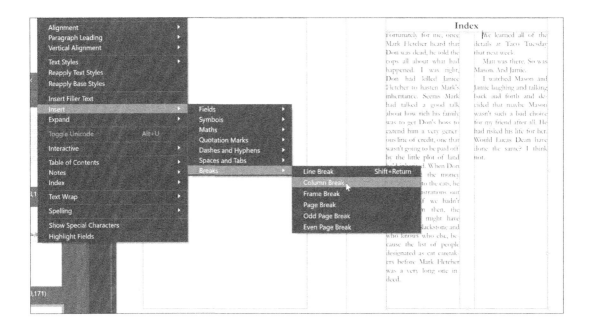

We're going to now use this for an index instead of basic text. So let's clear out that text and now learn how to insert an index.

INDEXES

An index lets you create a listing, generally at the back of your book, of where key subjects are discussed within the main body of the document. As far as I know, you only get one index per book. (Unlike tables of contents where you can have more than one throughout the book.)

I use these for most of my non-fiction titles, but because we already started Part 1 with a fiction title, I'm just going to go with that to show how this works.

I had an issue early on with my index entries in the original version of Affinity Publisher where I would try to flag an entry as an index entry and instead end up inserting an index at that point in my document, and when I tried to undo that it would crash Affinity. So that drives part of how I approach inserting an index in Affinity.

It may not be an issue anymore. But I don't think it hurts to do things this way either.

Okay. So what I do is find an entry towards the back of my book and mark it as an index entry.

MARK AN INDEX ENTRY

To do this, click on the Artistic Text Tool, select the text that you want to flag, go to the Index panel, and click on Insert Marker.

It should, and it did for me just now, bring up an Insert Index Mark dialogue box that contains that selected text as your Topic Name. Change the text if you need to, and then click on OK.

Sometimes in the past it would not include the text for me if I did this through the Index Panel, so you may have to manually type it in yourself, but hopefully that issue has been fixed in 2.0.

Your other option would be to go to Text→Index→Insert Index Mark or use Ctrl + Alt + Shift + [to insert an index mark. (I personally never use that control shortcut because it's just too much for me to remember each time.)

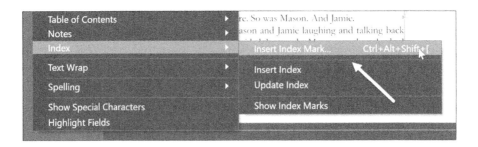

Note in the image above how Insert Index is right below Insert Index Mark? This is where I'd get myself in trouble, because I'd accidentally select Insert Index instead of Insert Index Mark.

To prevent that possibility, once you have a single index mark, go to where you want to place your index in your document, and insert it. Since you can only have one index in a document that will prevent you from accidentally inserting an index elsewhere.

INSERT AN INDEX

To insert an index in your document, click into the text frame where you want the index, and then go to the Index panel and click on the option for Insert Index at the top. It should be the fourth icon you see:

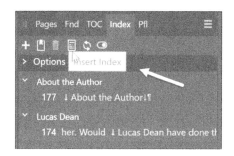

(You could also use the menu option I pointed out above.)

Affinity will insert an index into your document at that location. Like so:

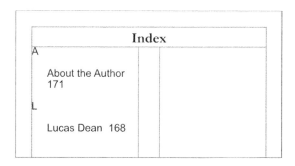

I only have two entries so far, so that's what you can see here.

Next, walk through the rest of your document, find text entries you want to add to your index, and create markers from them.

UPDATE INDEX

If you are lucky, the index will update automatically as you add new entries. For the last half dozen books I did, that's what happened for me. But just now while working on this index here, it didn't.

If your index does not automatically update as you add new entries, simply use the Update Index option at the top of the Index panel (the little arrows in a circle) to update the contents of the index.

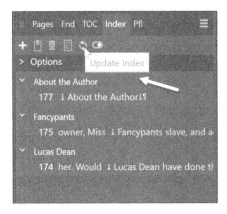

I don't really worry about it either way until I've flagged all of my entries. At which point you'll either get to the end and have a page or more of entries listed, or you'll get to the end and have that one single entry you started with.

If it's just the one, refresh. If they're all there, great, you don't have to do anything else.

I have yet to see a pattern as to when it works and when it doesn't. For me, the index is one of the less stable areas of Affinity Publisher.

SEE INDEX MARKS

The other item at the end of that top menu in the Index panel is a little toggle that lets you turn on and off index marks in your document. I usually keep that turned off, but if you weren't sure something had been flagged yet, you could turn that on to see.

It's very subtle. It's a light-gray-colored flag which you can (perhaps) see on the last line of this paragraph:

I watched Mason and Jamie laughing and talking back and forth and decided that maybe Mason wasn't such a bad choice for my friend after all. He had risked his life for her. Would Lucas Dean have done the same? I think not.

ADD TOPIC

Your other option at the top of the Index panel is on the far left and is a small plus sign. That lets you add a topic without adding an index marker. Click on it to bring up the Add Index Topic dialogue box:

I sometimes use this for topics like "Definitions" that aren't going to be directly-flagged entries. I can then flag individual entries such as Dialogue Box, Dropdown Menu, etc. and assign Definitions as the parent topic, which puts those individual entries as sub-topics under that heading.

Here, for example, I added "Characters" as a topic:

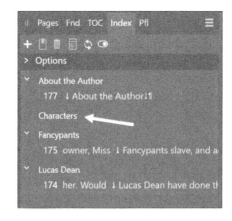

You can see that it has no flagged entries because there's no page number and text listed below it like for the other three.

MOVE INDEX ENTRY TO CREATE SUBTOPIC

If you want to move existing entries to be a sub-topic of another existing entry, you can left-click on the entry and drag to do so.

Here I left-clicked on Fancypants and dragged it to under the Characters topic. Now Fancypants is indented and shown as a sub-topic of Characters.

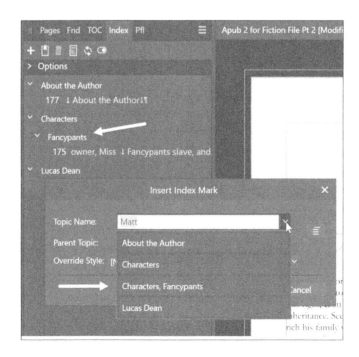

I also have the Insert Index Mark dialogue box showing here so you can see that Fancypants is now listed as "Characters, Fancypants". The first text listed is the highest level for the entry and then there's a comma and then the sub-entry text.

INSERT NEW ENTRY AS SUBTOPIC

For a new entry that you want to insert as a sub-topic, choose the topic name like you would for any other index entry, but then also use the Parent Topic dropdown menu to choose the associated main topic:

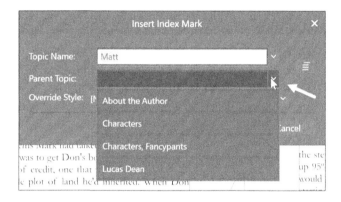

EDIT EXISTING ENTRY TO CREATE SUBTOPIC

Another way to assign a topic as a sub-topic is to right-click on the topic once it's listed in your index entries listing and choose to Edit Topic:

This will bring up the Edit Index Topic dialogue box which allows you to select a Parent Topic, like I did here with Characters:

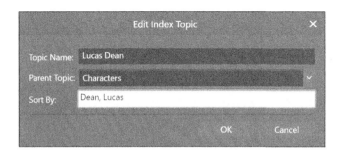

MOVE A SUBTOPIC TO PARENT TOPIC LEVEL

To move a subtopic up to its own level, right-click, choose to Edit Topic, and then delete the parent topic information and click on OK.

EDIT EXISTING ENTRY

You can also use the Edit Topic dialogue box to change the text for the Topic Name if needed.

Another option is to click on the name itself in the Index panel and edit it directly, but if you do so it will overwrite the whole name and you will have to type it all in from scratch.

CHANGE SORT ORDER FOR INDEX ENTRY

In the above image of the Edit Index Topic dialogue box you can see that in the Sort By field I typed in "Dean, Lucas". If you type a value into that field, Affinity will sort that index entry based upon the text in the Sort By field instead of the text in the Topic Name field.

In general you would use this for a situation where the Topic Name includes a word at the start like "the" that you didn't want to drive the sort order.

But you can see here that it worked in this instance as well because "Lucas Dean" is now sorted above "Fancypants":

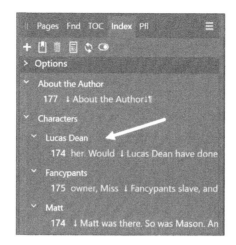

INSERT ANOTHER MARKER FOR THE SAME TOPIC

If you already have one entry for a topic, click anywhere on the word and click to insert a marker and you should see something like this where it selected the whole word and then suggested any existing topics that match that text:

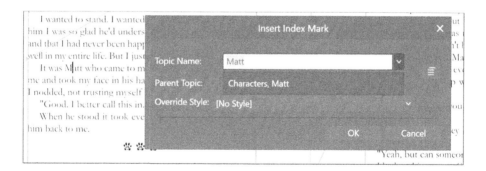

Click on that entry and the parent and topic name will all populate.

ASSIGN AN INDEX TOPIC TO A PAGE RANGE

If you want Affinity to list an index entry for a page range, flag each page in that range for that topic even if that word is not specifically used on that page. Just click somewhere on the page and insert a marker and then choose the marker you want from the dropdown menu.

Affinity will show a page range when you have two or more pages in a row flagged, like I did here:

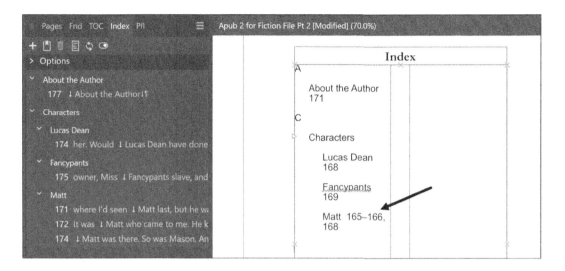

PAGE NUMBERS USED IN YOUR INDEX

Look at the page numbers in the image above.

The page number listed in the Index panel is the page number for the entire document, including any front matter. But the page number that is displayed in the actual index will match your page numbering in your document. So most likely the two will not match.

You can see above, for example, that "Lucas Dean" was flagged on page 174 of the document. But the index shows that as page 168 because that is the page number that a reader would actually see if they flipped through the book looking for that entry.

DELETE INDEX ENTRY

To delete an entry that you have listed for the index, just click on it and then click on the trash can at the top of the Index panel.

CROSS-REFERENCES

To create a cross-reference, for a new topic add that information in the See field: It will look like this:

If it's an existing topic, right-click and choose Add Cross Reference, and then

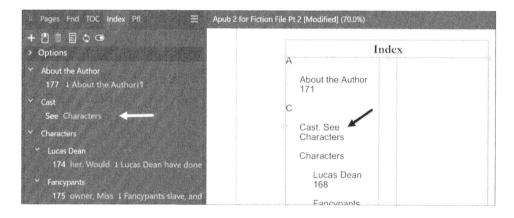

choose in the dropdown the topic to cross reference to.

FIND ALL INSTANCES OF INDEXED TERM IN DOCUMENT

Once you've added a topic, you can right-click on that topic and choose Find in Document from the dropdown. That will show you all instances of that word in the document:

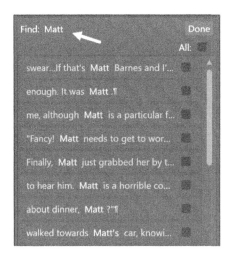

You can see the text around each usage if you're not sure you want to include an entry. Click on one of the entries to be taken to that page in the document and see the full text surrounding the use of the term.

ADD ALL INSTANCES OF INDEXED TERM TO INDEX

After searching for an indexed term, if you click the All box at top, all of those instances will be added as index entries for that topic. You can also check the individual boxes next to each entry to choose which ones to include.

Click Done when you're finished selecting which entries to include to return to the main view in the Index panel.

MANUAL CHANGES TO YOUR INDEX

Once you've inserted an index into your document it is possible to manually change that index and I have done so on occasion.

The default is for each letter of the alphabet that has an entry to display separately. So you can see here, for example, that M and N each only have one entry and display separately:

But at times that has pushed my index off to the next page in ways that I didn't like. Maybe I only had one entry on the last page. Or maybe the S category fell so that the S was on one page but all of its entries were on the next.

In those cases, I have manually combined the M and N categories to bring the text up.

But you have to be careful if you ever do that, because Affinity will overwrite that change if the index is updated after that point and Preflight will tell you that the index needs updated. So if you do a manual change like that, make it the last thing you ever do in that file.

Also, any spelling issues, etc. should not be fixed manually. Make those in the Index panel on that specific entry not in the index that you placed in your document.

TEXT STYLES

The index uses text styles so you can edit your entries to use your chosen font, etc. and then update that text style to carry that through all entries in the index.

Each level of the index uses a different text style, so requires separate formatting if you're going to change the font or other attributes from the default.

But this does allow you to have different formatting (like italics) on your sub-topics or sub-sub-topics.

MERGING MULTIPLE DOCUMENTS WITH INDEX ENTRIES

When you merge multiple documents that used an index, all of those markers will feed into the one document index so you will not have to redo all of that work. (Yay. Because creating an index for a two-hundred page non-fiction book can be hours of work.)

REUSING A FILE THAT HAD AN INDEX

If you ever reuse a file that had an index, be sure to go to the Index panel and see if there are still entries listed there. It is very likely you will have to select and delete them manually even if you've already deleted the pages of your document that had those entries or included the index.

I have found in the past that I also needed to do this a handful of entries at a time. It wouldn't let me delete all of my index entries at once. So I had to use Shift and click to select a range of entries and then use the trash can and keep doing that until they were all gone.

* * *

One final note on indexes. As I mentioned above, indexes have been the most glitchy part of Affinity for me. This is where Affinity is most likely to crash. Or where things just don't quite work the way they should. So I just want to encourage you to breathe deeply if you work with them and accept that things may not go smoothly. But trust me that using the Index panel is far better than trying to manually build an index yourself.

And, also, they seem to be constantly improving the product, so things are bound to get better. (Fingers-crossed.) Okay, on to images.

IMAGES

Alright. Now we're up to a key non-fiction topic, at least for the types of books I write, but one that may not be as relevant for those who write fiction, and that is placing images directly into your text.

If you're reading this book in print, you'll see probably a hundred examples of that in one book. I like to keep things simple so I have the text jump my images. That means I put an image on its own line. You don't have to do that. You can have text wrap around an image instead. And it may very well look better to do so, it just probably requires more time per image if you take that approach.

So. Let's get some images into our book and see how this all works. In Part 1 we had an accent image we used that was inserted directly onto a master page.

But what I've found works best for my books is to use a picture frame and bring my pictures into that frame instead. I'm going to show you a couple other options first, though.

Let's get a Text and Text page spread to work with. I went ahead and used Text→Insert Filler Text to get enough nice Latin gibberish for both frames. But I then had to copy that, paste it into Word, and then bring it back and paste it into Affinity to let it be editable. I also had to go to Text→Spelling→Check Spelling While Typing to turn off the spellcheck that had put a red squiggly line under every word.

But here we are, two text frames full of text:

Etiam ac augue. Morbi tincidunt neque ut lacus. Duis vulputate cursus orci. Mauris justo lorem, scelerisque sit amet, placerat sed, condimentum in, leo. Donec urna est, semper quis, auctor eget, ultrices in, purus. Etiam rutrum. Aliquam blandit dui a libero. Praesent tortor tortor, bibendum vehicula, accumsan sed, adipiscing a, pede. Nullam et tortor. Suspendisse tempor leo quis nunc fringilla volutpat. Donec rutrum ullamcorper lorem. Nunc tincidunt sagittis augue. Quisque lacinia. Phasellus sollicitudin.

Mauris purus. Donec est nunc, ornare non, aliquet non, tempus vel, dolor. Integer sapien nibh, egestas ut, cursus sit amet, faucibus a, sapien. Vestibulum purus purus, elementum ac, luctus ullamcorper, ornare vitae, massa. Nullam posuere sem ut mauris. Nullam velit. Quisque sodales. Donec suscipit suscipit erat. Nam blandit. Praesent congue lorem non dolor. Maecenas vitae erat. Ut ac purus vel purus dapibus gravida.

Nullam lorem sapien, tempus ac, fringilla at, elementum sed, purus. Duis molestie pede. Vivamus quis odio sit amet libero sodales tincidunt. Nam sit amet metus vitae lectus ullamcorper dignissim. Suspendisse leo. Praesent turpis justo, aliquet ac, accumsan vel, posuere quis, pede. Morbi pretium lacus. Cras non metus. Donec laoreet sem at elit. Cum sociis natoque penatibus et magnis dis parturient montes, nascetur ridiculus mus. Vivamus iaculis dolor id felis. Phasellus cursus nulla non odio. Nulla a lectus sed nisi luctus pretium. Sed egestas rutrum odio. Nunc ornare arcu. Quisque at augue ac magna sollicitudin sodales. Donec nulla justo, adipiscing sit amet, feugiat ac, facilisis euismod, risus.

Pellentesque tincidunt, dolor eu dignissim mollis, justo sapien iaculis pede, vel tincidunt lacus nisl sit amet metus. Fusce ac est vitae purus varius tristique. Phasellus mattis ornare ligula. Donec id nibh. Vestibulum metus quam, ultrices in, sagittis tincidunt, gravida et, sapien. Sed

174

bibendum, lectus vitae tincidunt dapibus, sem felis posuere est, id ornare augue lorem in purus. Suspendisse ligula. Sed mollis tristique mauris. Nullam nunc nunc, aliquet et, tristique nec, porttitor quis, urna. Etiam eu erat. Morbi ut nisl. Curabitur semper sem. Nulla turpis nibh, tempor nec, aliquet vitae, elementum ac, mauris.

Quisque pellentesque metus ac quam. Donec magna nulla, aliquet vitae, congue ac, faucibus ut, erat. Donec sit amet neque. Donec posuere tempus massa. Duis vulputate mauris sit amet purus. Duis vestibulum. Fusce ac erat. Curabitur sagittis. Pellentesque ultricies, ante id lobortis feugiat, ipsum magna congue risus, pulvinar euismod arcu nunc ac turpis. Cum sociis natoque penatibus et magnis dis parturient montes, nascetur ridiculus mus. Aliquam vel quam ut tellus gravida faucibus. Vivamus justo est, elementum vitae, malesuada eu, fermentum in, sapien. Donec sit amet justo. In velit. Vivamus turpis pede, dignissim sed, scelerisque nec, pretium sit amet, dui. Nam nec felis non turpis hendrerit varius. In ultrices ornare lorem. Quisque bibendum, massa sed venenatis malesuada, diam ipsum blandit urna, vel ultricies pede nulla vitae lacus.

Lorem ipsum dolor sit amet, consectetuer adipiscing elit. Quisque in augue. Donec aliquam magna nonummy enim. Proin blandit imperdiet sem. Donec malesuada, urna sit amet varius aliquam, nibh tortor laoreet turpis, eget sodales felis nibh ac sapien. Fusce eget augue. Integer sed risus. Aenean mollis. Donec facilisis egestas quam. Duis bibendum augue id mauris. Sed laoreet, tortor vel cursus fringilla, turpis elit vestibulum arcu, eu varius dolor leo in nulla. In sem ipsum, faucibus quis, varius tristique, porta eget, lorem. Curabitur hendrerit diam et mauris. Etiam porta nunc euismod dui. Maecenas a lectus. In hac habitasse platea dictumst. Suspendisse id massa. Nullam porta velit sed lacus. Duis eleifend, felis eu euismod lacinia, felis erat feugiat nisl, vitae congue leo velit a massa. Quisque nec justo a turpis posuere tristique.

175

I can now click at the beginning of that second paragraph and use the Place Image Tool to place an image. If I do so, this is what happens:

That screenshot of the Section Manager dialogue box inserted into my document at that point and at a size that made its resolution 300 DPI, which is the DPI I have specified for this document.

Here is another image inserted into the document at the same point using the Place Image Tool:

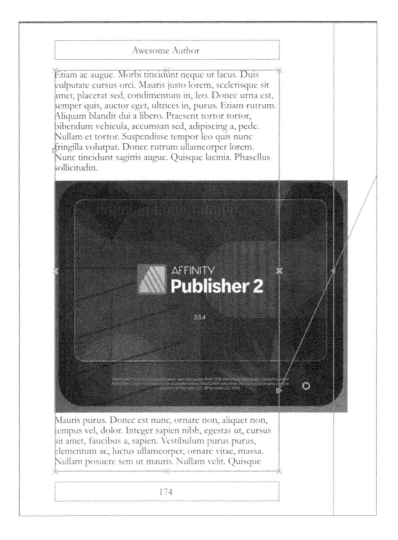

It also inserted at 300 DPI in accordance with my settings. (To see your DPI for your document, at least on a PC, go to File→Document Setup→Document and look at the specified DPI value.)

If you make that image smaller than it is right now, the DPI will go up. Make it larger, the DPI will go down. So that image as inserted into my document is as large as I can use, because for print you need a minimum DPI of 300.

(If you're ever struggling to get a higher DPI on your inserted images, chances are that you need a better display resolution to capture better images. Trying to fix it at this point is generally going to be too late in the process.)

You can see the DPI of an image in your document in one of two ways. Click on the Move Tool (the black arrow) and then click on the image layer in the

Layers panel. In the dynamic menu up top it will show the image name as well as its dimensions and DPI.

This image is 1468x1125 pixels and 300 DPI.

Your other option is to go to Window→Resource Manager. That will list all images in your document at once. Scroll to the right to see the placed DPI for each image:

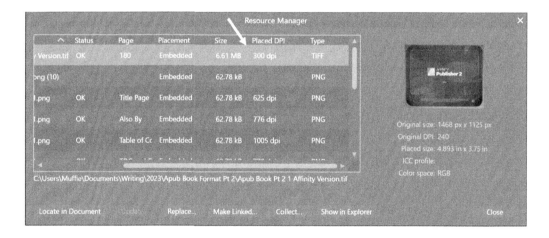

If you don't see a value there, like we don't for the second line, it's because the image is embedded in the document and used more than once. Expand that listing to see each usage and its corresponding DPI value.

The Resource Manager is the quick and easy way to see if any of the images in your document are below the minimum. Since my images come in at 300 DPI I generally don't have to worry about DPI as long as I only make images smaller and don't try to make them larger.

The two images above imported inline with the text. The good thing about an image that is inline with text (or pinned, which we'll discuss in a moment) is that it will move with the text.

Here I've inserted a different image at that same point and then changed my master page to Chapter Start and Text:

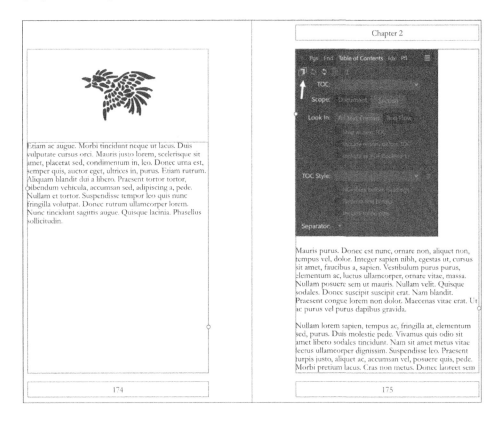

When the different formatting of the master page moved the text down, it took the image with it.

An image inserted inline into text acts like another line of text in the document and will move just like any line of text would.

In this case, the image is tall enough it had to move to the next page because there was no longer enough room for it on the first page. And because it's inline it has to fit in our text frame. I could make it smaller and it would move back to the first page, automatically.

Here we go:

Great. That image is always going to be between that first paragraph of text and that second paragraph of text. We like that.

But the reason I don't use it is because I don't like that appearance there. I want the image centered. And I personally struggle to get an image like that centered on the page.

You can open the Pinning panel (which we'll do in a moment) and go to the Inline tab and then change the Borders values to move the image from the left-hand edge of the text frame. It just never works well for me. It requires too much manual effort.

It's possible there is a way to do that easily, I've just never mastered it. The other issue I have with just directly inserting images is when I need a border around them. You can add a border to an inserted image using the Stroke option in the dynamic menu up top. Click on the white rectangle with a line through it and choose a line color and width.

But the challenge I've run into here in the past is that you had to do it for every single image separately. I just tested it and the good news is that the new Style Picker Tool will work to transfer a border from one image to another.

We covered that briefly in Part 1, but as a reminder, go to the Color Picker Tool towards the bottom of the list of tool options and click on the white arrow to expand the list to see the Style Picker Tool. Click on it. Click on the image with the border you want to copy, and then click on the image that you want to apply that border to, and the Style Picker Tool will also put a border around that second image.

So that makes using inline images less of a problem than it used to be for me before, but I still don't like trying to get an image placed on the page. This could be a me issue, not a them issue, so feel free to experiment.

The other option for placing an image that I also don't use is to pin the image. You can click on an image you've already placed and use the Float with Text option from the top menu or click on Float in the Pinning panel.

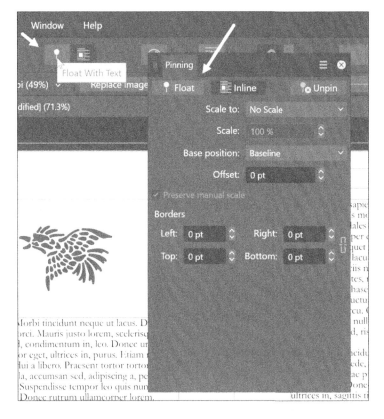

Both will convert the image from inline, which means it gets treated like a line of text, to pinned, which means it will still move with the text, but is not treated like a line of text. It sort of floats around near the text and you can move the "pin" that anchors the image to that text.

Here I've converted the second inserted image to Float and you can see that I was then able to click on it and drag it around but that there is a little blue pin with a line that connects that image to that point.

In the Pinning panel there are options for horizontal alignment of the image. Here I've used Inside Center of the text with an offset of 0 to place the image and it looks decent, but that took three adjustments to get that look:

Also, when I change the master page that applies here back to Text and Text, so move the text upward on the page, the image does move with the text, but see how it overlaps the text that comes after it:

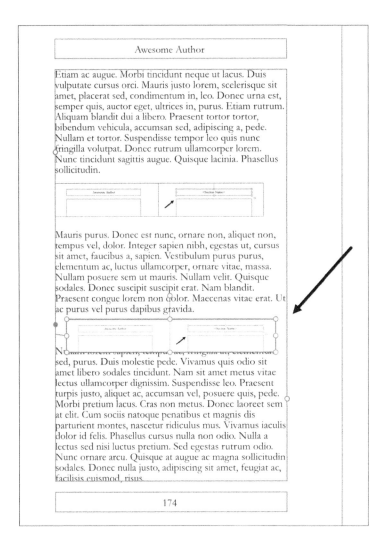

I could go in and adjust the Show Text Wrap Settings on that image to make the text jump the image to get rid of that overlap and then try to reposition it, but for me personally it's just a lot of effort involved when I have a better solution, which is using picture frames.

Now, to be clear, my method has flaws, too. If you add a bunch of text to your document, images in picture frames do not move, so you will have to manually reposition those images. But since I try to do all of my editing outside of Affinity, when I come to Affinity my text is final or almost final, so I can place my images without worrying that later edits will mean I have to reposition them.

Let me show you.

First off, as I write a document, I leave a note that the document needs an image at a specific point. Which means that when I drop my text into Affinity it looks something like this:

During the stage of book formatting when I'm walking through the document from start to finish and applying my master pages for chapter starts and looking for widows/orphans/short lines etc. that need fixing, I also insert my images.

The goal is to have every page final by the time I move on to the next.

Here I'd see that I need to insert an image and I would click on the Picture Frame Rectangle Tool:

Next, I would left-click and drag onto the document at about the point where it says I need an image until I have a rectangle showing on top of my text. Like this:

After the picture frame has been inserted into the document, I go to the Show Text Wrap Settings option up top and click on it to open the Text Wrap dialogue box. I then click on the Jump option:

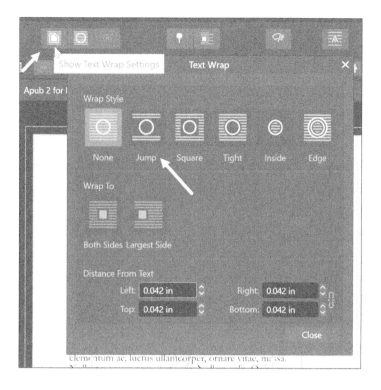

This should move the text that was under that picture frame rectangle to below the rectangle:

Now I can click on the Place Image Tool and find the image I want to bring in.

The image is going to come into the picture frame in various ways depending on your picture frame settings which can be found under Properties when you're clicked onto the picture frame:

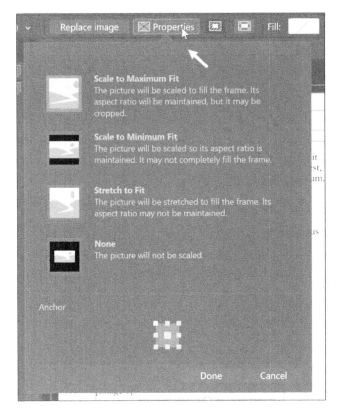

Scale to Maximum Fit is going to scale the image so that the picture frame is filled on either the horizontal or vertical axis, whichever makes more sense given the image shape compared to the picture frame shape. This means you may have part of the image out of frame.

Scale to Minimum Fit will scale the image so that it fits within the picture frame and is completely visible within the frame. But that means you will have space around the image if the image and the frame are not the exact same dimensions.

Stretch to Fit will stretch the image so that it fits within the picture frame. This will distort the image along one axis unless the frame and the image have the exact same proportions.

None just brings the image in at the document DPI, which in our case is 300. If you're going to use None, change that Properties setting before you bring the image in.

Here are all four used on the same image, I've added a border to the picture frames just so you can see them:

Top left is scaled to maximum fit. Below that is scaled to minimum fit. The top right is stretched to fit (and you can see the skew in the text that results). Below that is the None with our default DPI of 300. And across the bottom is how the image looks just dropped onto the page without using a picture frame.

For a document like we're creating here, I want to use None as my setting. That brings the image in at the largest possible size for the specified DPI, and I know that I can either use the image as-is or make it smaller from there.

Next step is to adjust the picture frame to the image. You can do that by clicking on Size Frame to Content in the dynamic menu up top:

From there you can adjust the frame and image size together using the blue circle located outside the perimeter of the frame in the bottom right corner. Just left-click on that circle and drag at an angle:

That should resize the frame and the image together.

You can use the slider underneath the frame to change just the image size, but if you do that it won't change the frame size and you'll have to click on Size Frame to Content once more to change the frame to fit the image.

(Or you could resize the image first and then size the frame to the content, but with a picture frame you're only going to see the part of the image that falls within the borders of the picture frame.)

You can also use the Transform panel to resize your image, just make sure to Lock Aspect Ratio when you do so to keep the image proportionate. (If you ever do stretch an image out of proportion Affinity will let you know that has happened in the Preflight panel.)

We want the frame and the image to be the same size because our next step, if it isn't already like this from using it before, is to add a border to the picture frame.

To do that, click on the frame and then click on the white rectangle next to Stroke in the dynamic menu up top. Next, go to the Swatches tab and click on the black swatch:

If the line isn't wide enough to be visible, you can adjust it by clicking on that white line to the right of the Stroke rectangle. That will open a dialogue box where you can then use a slider to adjust the line width or you can input a value for line width.

The nice thing about using a picture frame for this is that the next time you insert a picture frame in the document it will default to already having the same border that you used the last time and it will also default to the None import setting.

Which means that for all other images you insert into your document you just have to tell Affinity to jump the frame and then position it.

To position your image, click on the Move Tool and then left-click onto the picture frame and drag the image into position. You can also left-click onto the image and use the arrow keys to fine-tune your positioning.

I use the Snapping lines to make sure the image is centered in the middle of the text frame. Affinity will show center lines for both the overall page as well as just the text frame, so be sure you choose the center line for the text frame and not the overall page since the margins on book pages are uneven.

I usually do this visually, but if you bring the image in from the outer edge of the page, the first center line you encounter will be the correct one.

If you have multiple images on a page, sometimes it helps to hide the other images while centering an image. To do that, click on the little gray circle for that image layer in the Layers panel. It will turn a darker gray color when the layer is hidden as you can see here:

Just be sure to unhide the image again afterward by clicking on that circle once more.

Once an image is centered left to right, you can also move it up and a down a bit using the arrow keys to see where it's best to place it between the lines of text. I usually find that there is a spot that results in equal distance between the line above and the line below.

Also, sometimes you can "push" the text below the image down one line or "raise" it one line by moving the image slightly, but you can only move an image so far before more text jumps the image, so watch out for that. The line that is meant to be below the image will suddenly be above it or vice versa.

Note that this will work somewhat differently if you choose to wrap text around the picture frame rather than jump it.

238

Finally, my last step is to delete that text that says [Image 1] because I no longer need it to tell me to insert that image. I also often will format the paragraph below an image to remove the indent from that paragraph, but that's a matter of personal preference.

Note that when I'm doing this I am moving back and forth between using various tools. So when I'm moving a picture frame around I have the Move Tool selected but when I delete the text that said [Image 1] I have to click on the Artistic Text Tool before doing that. So if something isn't working for you, check that you have the right tool selected.

Now, one other issue to address here when using picture frames to put images into your document is that the picture frame will stay where you put it. The frame is not tied to your text. If you insert text in your chapter and that moves the rest of the text down, you'll need to also manually move any picture frames past that point to account for that.

But more commonly the issue is that the text does not naturally fall in a way that works with the picture frame.

Let's look at an example here of what I mean. I need to insert another image here where it says Image 2:

But the image I need to insert is too big for the space that's left at the bottom of the page. Here I've brought it in at the top of the next page where it can actually fit:

The problem is, the text is still on the other page, because of the way the text naturally flows across the text frames. To fix this, I have to manually add a frame break to push the text from [Image 2] onward to the next page.

I covered that in the last book, but as a reminder, click where you want the break, and go to Text→Insert→Breaks→Frame Break.

This will push all of that text forward to the next text frame. Delete the placeholder text and you end up with something like this:

You could also explore other options in a scenario like this. I will sometimes see if I can move an explanatory paragraph above the image instead of having it below the image, for example, if the gap is really big. Or I may make other images a little smaller earlier in the chapter if that helps me bring an image to the bottom of the prior page. Or, if there's room to do so, I might increase the size of an image a bit to push text down.

But sometimes (as you've seen if you have the print version of this book) I just leave that white space there.

Another option that I don't use is to change the text wrap setting. I always jump the image, but you could have the text wrap around the side of the image instead, especially for any image that only takes up a small part of the page.

Like here where I've set the text to wrap around the larger side of an image and moved the image to the left-hand side of the text frame:

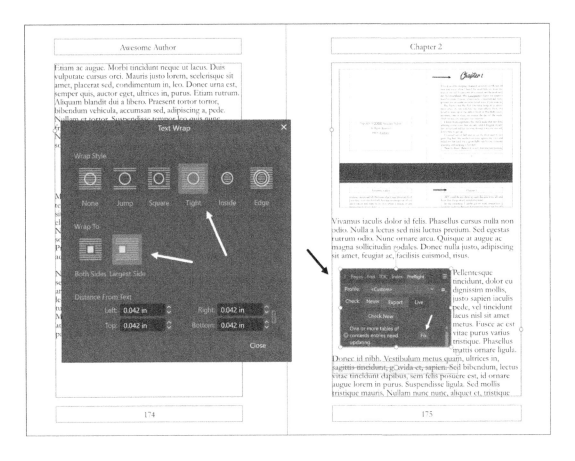

* * *

One final note that I'm adding to the end of this chapter: When I was formatting the first book in this series in Affinity I noticed that sometimes my picture frame setting would reset from None to Scale to Maximum Fit and the next image I imported into the picture frame was the wrong dimensions. To fix this I'd Undo and then change the Properties setting back to None.

I suspect the reason this happened a handful of times was because I accidentally clicked on the Clear Fill on Populate option which is in the dynamic menu right next to the Size Frame to Content option. So I'm adding a caution here to be sure you don't click the wrong option. And, if you do, to let you know you just need to go and change that Properties setting back to None once more.

Also, I wanted to more specifically mention here that when you're working with a picture frame and add an image to that frame that the image will be its own layer underneath that frame. If you go to the Layers panel and expand the picture frame layer you'll see a listing for the image underneath. You can click on that image layer to adjust just the image, but will then need to adjust the frame as well after the fact. I try to stay at the picture frame layer level as much as possible because that should adjust them both, but there have been times I needed to drop down to the image layer instead, so I wanted to let you know that's possible.

This is especially likely to be needed if you change the picture frame dimensions using the Transform panel, because the dimensions of the underlying image may not change to match.

Okay, so that was placing images in your document, now let's talk about adjusting them.

IMAGE ADJUSTMENTS

This may be something I am doing wrong, but I found with my setup using the greyscale 8 setting in Affinity (as recommended by IngramSpark) and then generating as a PDF and sending off to Amazon KDP or IngramSpark, that my images needed to be manually adjusted to print well.

Images that are mostly white with black lines I have to darken and images that are mostly black I have to lighten.

You may have a different experience. I would recommend ordering a proof copy the first time you generate a book in black and white that has a lot of images using Affinity to see what your specific outcome is.

I am by no means an expert on image adjustment. I think there are people out there who manually adjust every single image in a book with detail and care. Me, I say, "that's a lighter image, let's darken it up some" and "that's a darker image, let's lighten it up some."

What you decide to do will be up to you, but let me see if I can't demonstrate this for you.

Below is a darker image from earlier in the book, unadjusted first and then adjusted:

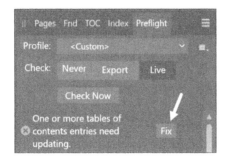

For the ebook you are seeing a screenshot of this. You can see that the lower image is more gray than black and I personally think the text is a little bit more visible.

Here is the same thing for a lighter-colored image that I've darkened:

In this case I think the lines come out darker in the second image than the first which makes them a little easier to see.

This is a matter of personal preference. You may disagree with the adjustments or think I didn't take them far enough. Or think there's a better way to adjust them.

But let me show you what I'm doing here. Go to the Layers panel and click on the layer for the image you want to adjust.

At the very bottom of the Layers panel, you will see a trio of icons:

The one I use is for Adjustments. Click on that to see a dropdown menu (that drops upward) that lists a large number of potential adjustments you can apply. The one I use is Brightness and Contrast. Clicking on that opens a Brightness/Contrast dialogue box:

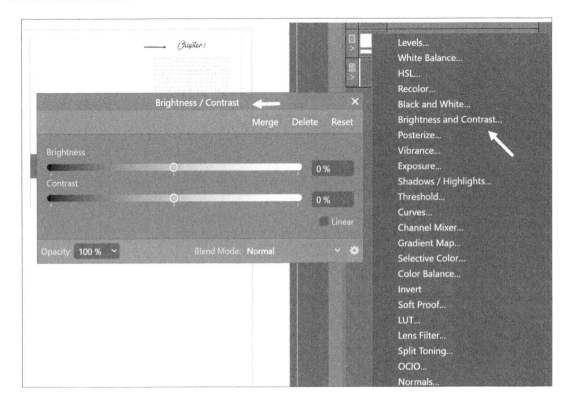

I then either change the brightness value to 35% for dark images or -25% for light images.

Again, I will remind you that I probably do not do this in an ideal way. But if you're reading this in print and could read the images to this point, it worked well enough.

Once you've added an adjustment to a layer, it will show as part of that layer in the Layers panel:

If you click on the little arrow on the left-hand side of the layer to expand it, you can then click on the icon for the adjustment to open that dialogue box once more.

You can also right-click on the adjustment layer and delete it. Or if you want to keep the adjustment but remove it for now, click on the gray circle at the end of the layer row to hide the adjustment.

There is another way to reach the adjustment options and that is through the menu up top. Click on your layer and then go to Layer→New Adjustment→Brightness/Contrast from there.

As you can see in that dropdown menu there are a lot of other image adjustment options available.

There is also a Layer Effects dialogue box. You can open it by using the right-most of those three icons at the bottom of the Layers panel or by going to Layer→Layer Effects.

The Layer Effects dialogue box lets you add shadows, glow, color overlays, etc. I find I use the Layer Effects for cover design or ad images, but not for simple images in book layouts. I'm just mentioning it here so that you know about it.

So, to summarize images. You have three options for placing images in the main body of your document. I prefer to use picture frames. If you use those, insert the picture frame, change the settings so that your text jumps the frame, bring in the image using the None setting, resize as needed and fit the frame to the picture, place the image using your Snapping lines, and then adjust the brightness of the image as desired.

Okay. On to the messiest topic, combining files to create a collection or omnibus.

MERGE MULTIPLE BOOKS

The way I typically will build a book that contains more than one book is to start with the first book in the collection. So let's do that.

I created these books in the original version of Affinity, so it gives me a warning message when I try to open the file:

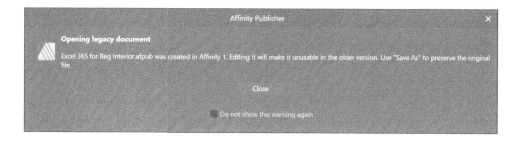

Make sure you have a copy of the original saved somewhere just in case if that happens to you.

Okay. First step is to insert a new title page after the first two page spreads. (Depending on the front matter of your book, you may want to insert the new title page somewhere else. For me, I like to put it after the also by listing but before the table of contents.)

I right-click on pages 2 and 3 of the document and choose Add Pages.

I want 2 pages, After, page 3, using the Title Page master page.

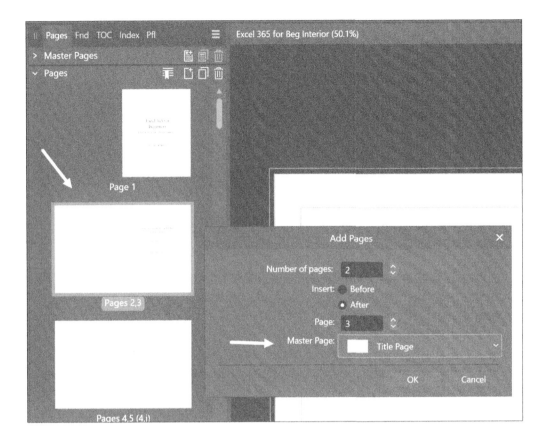

Now select the Artistic Text Tool and go to the first page, the original title page of the document, and copy the text in that text frame. Go back to the newly-inserted title page and paste that text into the text frame there.

Once that's done, you can go back to page 1 and change the title information there to the name of the collection.

(I find it easier to do it this way rather than insert a new Title Page at the beginning of the document because that first page being just a right-hand page has given me interesting results in the past when I tried to insert pages before it.)

Next step is to review the copyright notice and also by pages. For me, I need to update my copyright notice with the new ISBN and year.

After that, we need to insert a new table of contents page spread for the entire collection. I want to place that table of contents in front of the new title page for the first book but after my also by page, and I'm going to leave that blank for the moment.

Here we are. This is our new front matter:

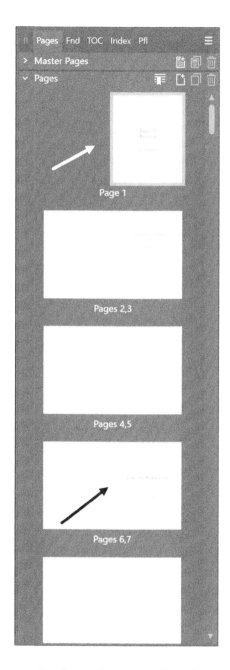

You can see the first page is the title page for the collection, followed by a copyright and also by page spread, followed by a table of contents for the collection, followed by a title page spread for the first book, and then the table of contents for the first book.

That's the easy part. Now we have to go to the end of this book and delete out any back matter that more appropriately belongs at the end of the collection. And we need to leave a left-hand page for the last page spread so that the next book comes in appropriately, because Affinity treats the first page spread in each book as just a single-page spread. So if you don't have a page to push that first page to start on the right the whole next book will be on the wrong side of the page.

Here is the back matter I need to delete:

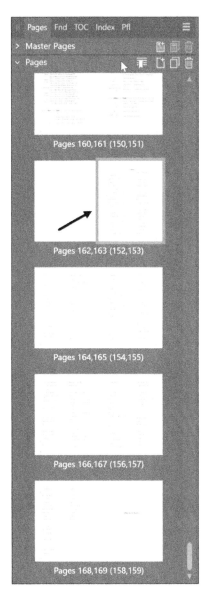

Pages 153 through 159 which include my Index and my About the Author.

After you delete pages from the back of your document, check that you have no text overflow markers in your main text. On occasion I will have my text flow through to my about the author section. When I do that it becomes a problem if I then delete the about the author page, because the text is still there. Just because I took the page where you could see the text away that did not erase that text.

This is why I usually try to keep my about the author page and any back matter separate from the main body of my book. But I am not perfect and sometimes I mess that up. So check for the little red marks along the perimeter of your text frames in the main body of your book to see if this is an issue you need to fix.

If it is, I find the easiest way to fix it is to Undo and bring back the pages I just deleted, delete that text from the about the author page, and then delete the pages again.

You can also just click into the last text frame now available and start deleting text until there's no longer an indication of hidden text that's overflowing the frame. But that's harder because you're working blind and don't know how much to delete. Okay.

So delete the pages that are back matter. Also delete any note that might be at the end of this book telling readers the next book to read. (Something I do in my fiction titles.)

At that point, you should have something that looks like this:

Note the blank left-hand page at the end.

Right-click on that page and choose Add Pages from File from the dropdown menu.

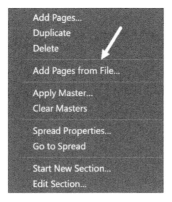

This will bring up an Open dialogue box. Find the next file you want to bring in and click on Open.

That will bring up the Add Pages dialogue box:

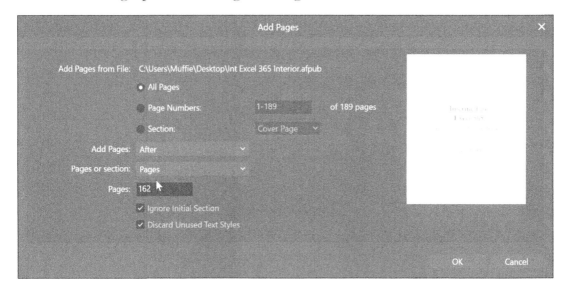

I choose to bring in All Pages, After the last page of my section. There is a checkbox there where Affinity can be told to Ignore Initial Section if you don't want your front matter, but I choose to bring it in because it has my title page. I also leave Discard Unused Text Styles checked because combining files can get messy when it comes to text styles and the less you have to deal with the better.

So basically I don't change anything here, I just click on OK.

Most likely the next thing you will see is an Imported Text Styles dialogue box which is going to show you text styles that Affinity is bringing in from the new file that aren't in the existing one. It will also indicate when there is a conflict, so two text styles with the same name that don't match exactly:

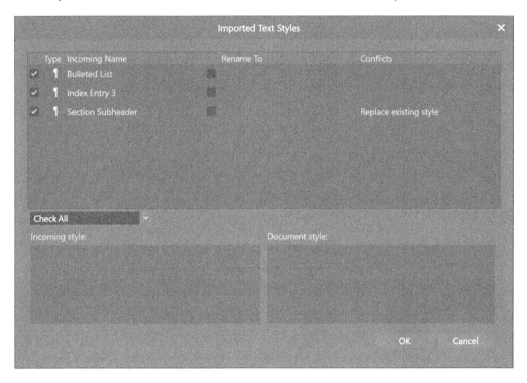

In the dialogue box above you can see that I had a bulleted list text style that is only used in the second book as well as a third-level Index Entry text style only used in the second book. Those are fine and don't require any sort of decision.

But the third line is telling me that I used different formatting for my section subheader between the two books. I don't want to have one overwrite the other because it could impact my text placement which is going to impact my page breaks and images, potentially.

So I click on the Rename To box and Affinity assigns that section subheader text style that's being brought in a unique name:

Great. Now I know that both books will be formatted the way they were originally. I can scan through later and see if the difference between the two subheaders is so noticeable it needs to be changed, but in this case it's likely not going to be a problem.

The folks at Affinity envision this merging different files option as something to use for group collaboration. In that case, where it's different sections of one book being brought together, you probably would want to overwrite one or the other text style rather than keep both.

Okay. Done.

Affinity brings in my entire second book and because I had that single blank left-hand page at the end, the title page, etc. are all where they should be:

For this one, I need to delete the individual book copyright notice. (I used to leave them in but Amazon made me remove them at some point so now I just have the collection copyright page but not individual pages for the individual books.) I also don't need the also by information, so that entire spread can go.

That leaves me the title page for book two, the table of contents for book two, and then the rest of book two.

At the moment the page numbering is going to be off, because this book is set to restart page numbering at the first chapter. I'm going to fix this later. But keep in mind it's an issue.

I now get to rinse and repeat for as many additional books as I want to add to this collection, omnibus, what-have-you until I've added all of the books I want to include.

I only had one more to add, so I dropped it in, deleted the copyright and also by pages, and that was it. I leave the backmatter of the last book in place.

But what if you didn't have a book that conveniently ended with a left-hand page? How do you get one single page when you've been using two-page master pages?

What I do is insert a new page spread at the end that includes a blank left-hand page. So a No Text and whatever master page:

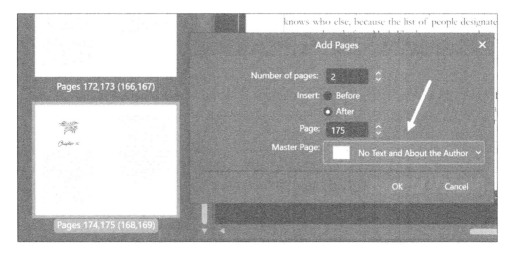

Next, I select just the right-hand page and right-click and choose to Delete it.

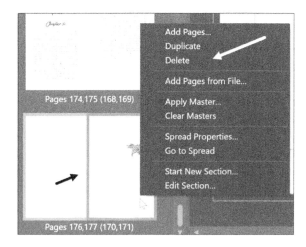

Note how the blue border showing which pages are selected is only around the right-hand page.

Okay, back to this other book we were formatting. Now that I have all my content in one book it's time to make it all work together.

The first thing to consider is how you had structured your chapter headers. I'm in luck with this one because it's a non-fiction title, which means I already had my headers formatted to use the chapter name. That means I don't have to make any adjustment there.

If you were instead using the book title, which you probably would do for most fiction titles, then you'll need to update your master pages to use section names and create sections for each book you imported and assign the book title as that section name.

Here, for example, is the Section Manager for a collection of three novels and a short story of mine:

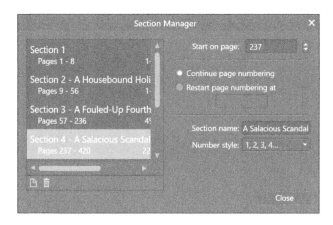

I have the third title selected here. You can see that each story or novel has its own page range assigned and the section name listed is the title of the novel or short story. Also, note that the page numbering is set to continue, not restart.

So do that if you need to do it for your book. Set each section name to match the book in question and while you're there check to continue page numbering through the whole book.

For mine, which is already fine in terms of the header, I need to go to the front matter for each individual title after the first title and make sure that all of those sections continue page numbering.

I right-click on any thumbnail in my book and choose Edit Section to bring up the Section Manager. (That's easier than trying to locate the start of each book in a five-hundred page document.) I can then scroll through the section listing on the left-hand side and look for any numbering listed on the right of that entry that is either in Roman numerals or restarts at 1:

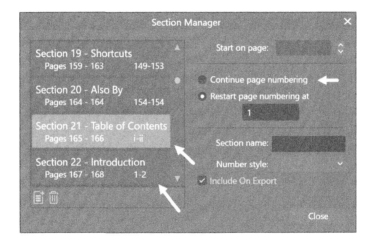

Here you can see the table of contents for the second book I added, for example. Section 21 is the table of contents for that book and currently it's using Roman numerals and also restarted the page numbering. Section 22 is the first chapter of that book which restarted page numbering at 1.

Both of those sections need to be edited to Continue Page Numbering and/or use the 1, 2, 3, 4, etc. numbering style. So I click on each one and make those changes.

Good news is that once I change Section 22 to continue page numbering, the rest of that book's page numbering will be fine because all other sections in the book were already set to continue page numbering.

So it's usually only two sections at most per book that was added that need to be updated. But be sure to scroll through the entire listing of sections to see if that page numbering on the right-hand side is continuous from page 1 of your document to the end.

The next step is for books that use an index. You should have left in the index for the last book you added. Go to the Index panel and look at your entries:

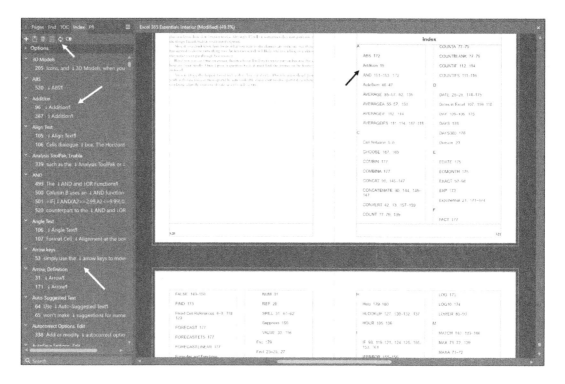

I can tell by the page numbers listed next to the entries in the panel that there are entries listed for all three of my books. The fact that I have some there with page 53 and some with page 367 means that the entire book is covered.

But note that the Index in the document itself is only showing entries right now for the last book. 3D Models, for example, are listed in my Index panel but not my document.

Easy enough to fix, just hit refresh at the top of the Index panel. But note that because you're combining multiple books that may push your index past the number of pages you had allotted to it for the last book:

See the red circles along the perimeter of the text frame there. These indicate that I have more index entries than text frames for them to flow to.

Which means I need to insert a new page spread (or more than one) for index entries and then flow the existing entries to them.

In this case, I had to add ten more pages to the index. I could have deleted my Also By and auto-flowed my text and Affinity would have done it for me, but I did it manually and flowed the text manually as well.

If you have an index, you should also read through it at the end and make sure that you have no situations where you used Definition, Select in one book but Select, Definition in another or anything similar where the entries need to be combined and streamlined.

If so, make those updates in the Index panel just like you would with a singular book.

Also, this is another reminder of why making custom edits to an index should be avoided as much as possible. Because any edits like that you did in the individual books were lost when you refreshed this index.

Okay, next up, tables of contents.

With novels that don't have named chapters, you're probably in luck because the only table of contents you need is at the front and is the title of each book. If you have a title page that lists the title, that's going to be very easy to create, you just need to know the Text Style that was used for that. In my case that text style is Book Title.

But if you used a cover image for your title page, that may be trickier. In that case, I'd recommend creating a text frame on that title page, typing your title into the frame, and assigning a text style to that title that you can use to feed a table of contents. You can then either hide that layer by clicking on the gray circle in the Layers panel or you can left-click and drag on that layer in the Layers panel to place it below the layer that contains the cover image.

Basically, create a layer on that page that has your title so Affinity can use it to create the table of contents, but then hide it somehow so it doesn't print on that page.

I do not recommend manually creating a table of contents.

Okay, so let's go build my main table of contents for this non-fiction book because there's one more trick I need to show you.

I want to go to page 5 of my overall document, click into the text frame, open the Table of Contents panel, and click on the Insert option.

Once Affinity has inserted a "no table of contents entries found" message on the page, I can then click on Book Title to bring in the title of my three books into my table of contents.

I have one issue, though, which is the Index and About the Author don't use that format. They both use the Chapter Title format. If I want to include them in my table of contents at the beginning (and also not have them listed in the table of contents for the last book), I need to assign them a new text style.

It can be identical to the chapter title style. It just needs to have a different name.

So I go to the first page of the Index, click on the header text at the top of the frame (Index), go up to the dropdown for the text style, and choose to create a new style. I'm going to call that new text style Backmatter.

Once I've created that new text style, I can then go to my About the Author page, click onto that text at the top of the frame, and assign the Backmatter text style to that one as well.

As far as a reader is concerned, my Index and About the Author text will match my chapter header text. But as far as Affinity is concerned, they use different text styles, so I can have a table of contents pull in those two entries without pulling in all of my chapter titles, too.

Now I can go back to that first table of contents and check the box to include any entries that use the Backmatter text style in the table of contents.

Because this is a new table of contents I also need to change the formatting for the entries in the table of contents to use Garamond and small caps. Small caps can be applied through the Typography section of the Character panel as can all caps.

Be sure to update those text styles as soon as you make that change.

I also need to tell Affinity to show page numbers. (If you update your text formatting in your table of contents but don't update the text style and then click on the option to show page numbers, Affinity will revert to the original text style.)

If you use more than one text style to populate your table of contents, like I have here, both will need to be formatted and updated separately.

And here we are:

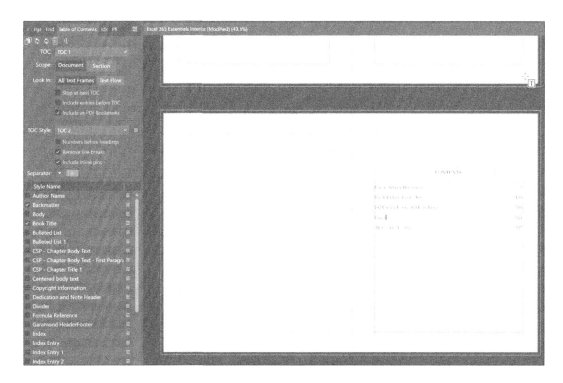

If you look on the left-hand side you can see that this is TOC 1, it does not stop at the next TOC, and it uses Backmatter and Book Title for the text styles that feed the table. Also, in the main document you can see that I've formatted the text and included page numbers.

That was the easy one.

Now we need to go to the next table of contents, which for me is on page 9 of my document. I should be able to click onto that table of contents and my Table of Contents panel should switch over to reflect that I'm now editing TOC 2. But I have had it in the past not be so reliable. So always check that TOC dropdown at the top of the Table of Contents panel before you start making changes.

This table of contents needs to be set so that it stops at the next TOC or else it will list all chapters in the entire document, which we don't want. (The other way to get around that would be if each document had different text styles assigned to those chapters, but I don't do that.)

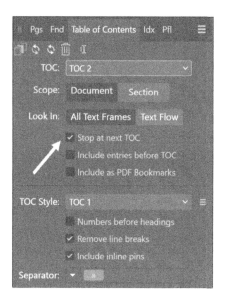

The Style Name should already be set to the correct text style from when you imported it.

If the table doesn't update automatically, then you will want to update it manually. Now, one thing to keep in mind when updating a table of contents is that you have two options available:

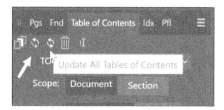

The first one, if you hold your mouse over it, just says Update. The second one says Update All Tables Of Contents. Be careful when you have multiple tables of contents to use the Update option not the Update All. (No matter which option you use, you'll want to go back through the document at the very end and check all of your tables of contents anyways, but if you get one working it is best to leave it alone.)

Okay, so I did that. The next step is to scan the entries and see if there's anything there that shouldn't be or any formatting that needs to be fixed, etc.

Good news is I have formatted table of content entries, they stop at the end of this particular title, and the chapter names look like what they should.

But, I have an issue:

It's showing an entry for index and it shouldn't be.

We deleted the index from this one. We changed the index text style at the end of the entire book. And we're stopping at the next table of contents. So somewhere in my first document here, there is hidden text for index that is formatted as a chapter title and I need to track it down and delete it and then update this table of contents.

Also, as soon as I fix that issue I will need to change the master page spread here to a No Text and Chapter Start master page since my table of contents will fit on just one page.

The best way to find a hidden entry is to use the Find and Replace panel. When I did that, it took me to the top of the title page for the second book I added:

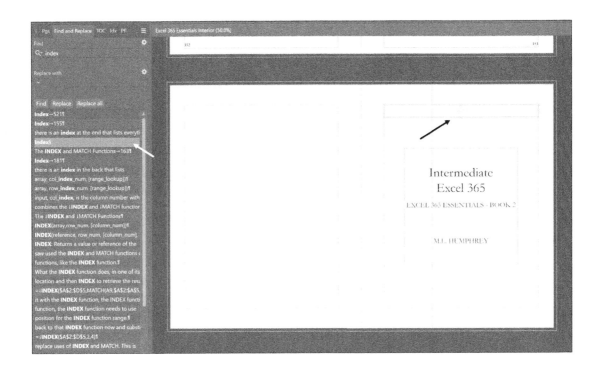

Sometimes weird things will happen with text in Affinity and instead of flowing to the next main body text frame it will flow to a header or footer text frame. It doesn't happen often and usually when it does I can undo and reverse it. But on this one I didn't notice, so now I have to try to fix it some other way.

I cheated to fix it, but it wasn't the ideal solution because that weird text is still hanging out in my document. But since the text was hidden I just selected that search result and changed the assigned text style to none. That meant it was no longer pulled into my table of contents.

Another solution that worked was to reapply the Title master page to that page spread because it should've never had a header so something was wrong there anyway.

Both approaches worked. I updated my table of contents, changed that master page spread, and was ready to move on to table of contents number three.

Okay. Let's do the next table of contents. You can see here that the page numbering needs to update since it currently shows page 1 for the first chapter:

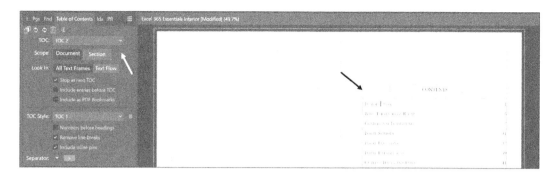

This time when I clicked onto what should be the third table of contents the TOC dropdown menu continued to show TOC 2. I had to manually change the dropdown to TOC 3. So always know which table of contents you're working on in your document and make sure the listed table of contents in the Table of Contents panel matches.

Once I did that and checked the box for "stop at next TOC" it updated just fine, which meant I could move on to the fourth and final one.

That one I also had to change the dropdown in the Table of Contents panel and then it updated fine.

But this was one that I had manually fixed something in for the first book and that issue came back:

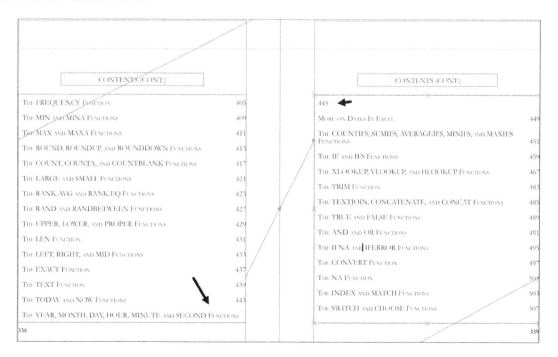

When your chapter names are really long, which mine sometimes are, that is going to impact your table of contents. As you can see here, it pushed the page number to the next line for this chapter. Also, since the page number was now on its own line it is on the left-hand side of the page.

If I click into that line and just type a handful of spaces, that pushes the page number to the right. But I still have the issue that the chapter name is on one page and the page number for that chapter is on the next.

Usually I'd try to fix the chapter name if it was me just being a little too verbose, but in this case that doesn't work. So I'm going to have to manually fix this by clicking into the table of contents and adding an enter to push the chapter listing to the next page:

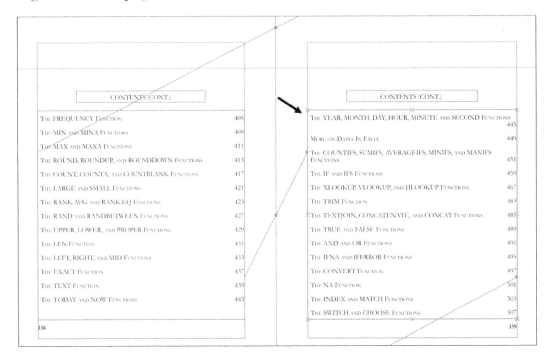

That works fine, but the problem is if I update that table of contents or accidentally choose to update all table of contents, I lose that change. So that edit is probably the absolute last thing I want to do in this document and I need to remember to ignore the Preflight warning that will suggest that I update my table of contents.

At this point we're pretty much done with merging these documents. The next step is to export as a PDF and then page through the entire merged document and look for any issues.

The main issues to check for are that the page numbering continues from the beginning chapter of the first book through to the last page continuous and uses the 1, 2, 3, 4, etc. style. That only necessary front and back matter pages are included. That the back matter is applicable for all of the books and has been updated accordingly. That each book starts on the correct page. That images, if used, are included and in the right location. That all headers and footers are accurate. That any master pages that needed updated have been updated. That all tables of contents in the document are updated and accurate. That the index, if one exists, has been updated and has no similar but not identical entries. And that there are no overflowing text frames anywhere.

MISCELLANEOUS

There are a few tips, tricks, etc. that I didn't cover in the earlier chapters that I want to quickly mention here.

TABLE OF CONTENTS SEPARATOR

By default the table of contents is going to list your text entries on the left-hand side and your page numbers on the right-hand side with a tab as the separator and blank space between the two.

But you can change this.

The Separator option in the Table of Contents panel has a dropdown menu that lets you choose a tab, bullet, em dash, en dash, em space, en space, or any combination of the above. You can also manually add text to that field.

Here, for example, is the main table of contents we used above now using a space, an em dash, and another space to separate the titles from the page numbers:

I typed the space, selected the em dash, and then typed the other space into that field, indicated by the arrow in the image above.

Be sure to hit Enter after you choose your separators or it will revert back to the default.

Another one that a lot of people like to use is a dotted line that connects the chapter title and page number. That needs to be applied from the Edit Text Style dialogue box.

Click on the text for one of your chapter listings in the table of contents, go to the Text Styles panel, right-click on the text style being used, and choose Edit [Style Name] from the dropdown menu:

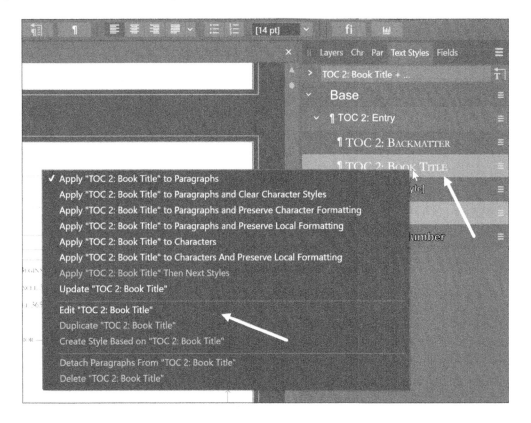

This will bring up the Edit Text Style dialogue box. Go to the Tab Stops option on the left-hand side under Paragraph. If there isn't already a tab stop listed, add one by clicking on the plus sign at the bottom of the black box in the center of the screen:

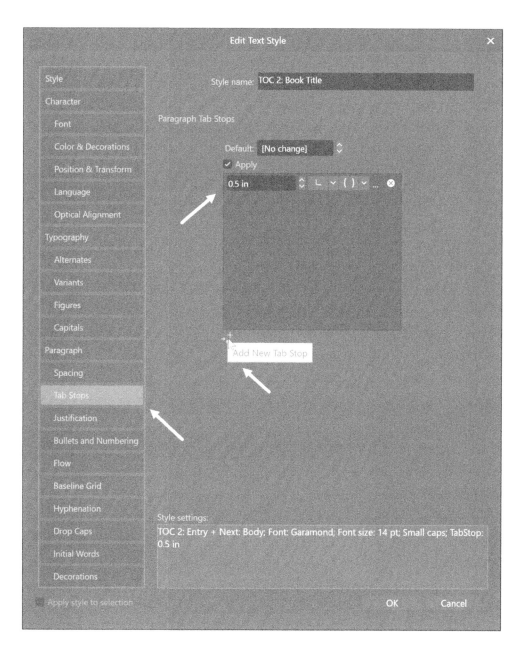

Once you have a tab stop you'll need to change the dropdown for Tab Stop Leader.

Use Character (.) if you want a dotted line, Underline (_) if you want a solid line that is at underline height, or Strikeout (-) if you want a solid line at midlevel.

You also need to use 0 for the listed numeric value and a right tab stop in the first dropdown menu (which you can see in the screenshot above).

Also, and I think this is new in Affinity Publisher 2.0, it didn't work for me until I changed the Separator in the Table of Contents panel to Right Indent Tab from a regular tab separator:

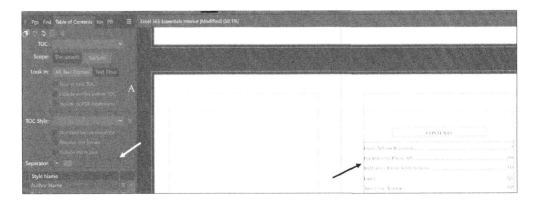

In the image above I've made this change for the chapter titles text style (the first three entries) but not the backmatter text style (the last two entries) so you can see the difference.

EXPORT IMAGE HEAVY BOOKS TO PDF

When I'm just using an accent image in a book in Affinity I export as a PDF/X-1a:2003 file. But for really image-heavy books I use custom settings.

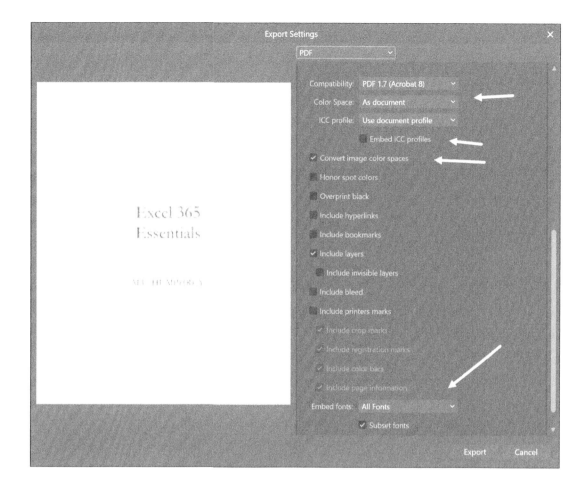

In the Advanced section for Export Settings, I use Compatibility of PDF 1.7, choose a Color Space of "as document", and an ICC profile of "use document profile".

I also make sure that the Embed ICC profiles box is not checked but I do check the Convert Image Color Spaces box. Finally, I make sure that Affinity will include Layers and embed all fonts.

Again, I may not be the expert here, but these settings have worked good enough for me. If you're spending a lot on a print run rather than doing print on demand, work with your printer on exactly what they need. (And if you're really curious, IngramSpark does publish a technical guidelines document that you can try to use as a guide.)

SAVE AN EXPORT PRESET

Because Affinity has the nasty habit (maybe not anymore, but it used to) of defaulting to the last export setting you used, not just for that document but for any Affinity document, I save my black and white export settings as a preset.

To do that, click on the three lines at the top of the Advanced section for a PDF export in the Export Settings dialogue box and choose Create Preset.

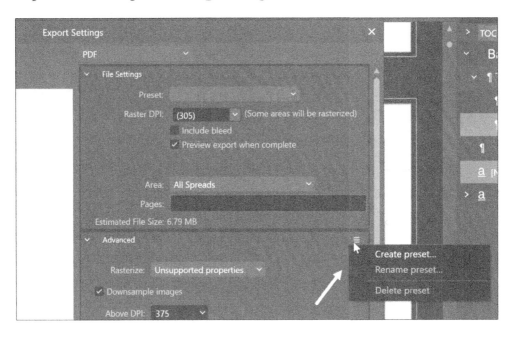

Give the preset a name when the dialogue box appears and click OK. It will then be available in your Preset dropdown menu so that you never have to think about it again.

CREATE A KEYBOARD SHORTCUT

You can create custom keyboard shortcuts in Affinity.

For example, I have a keyboard shortcut that automatically opens the Brightness/Contrast setting so that all I have to do to adjust an image is click on it, use my shortcut, and then input my adjustment value. I also recently added one for frame breaks.

To add a keyboard shortcut, go to Edit→Preferences to open the Preferences dialogue box, and click on Shortcuts.

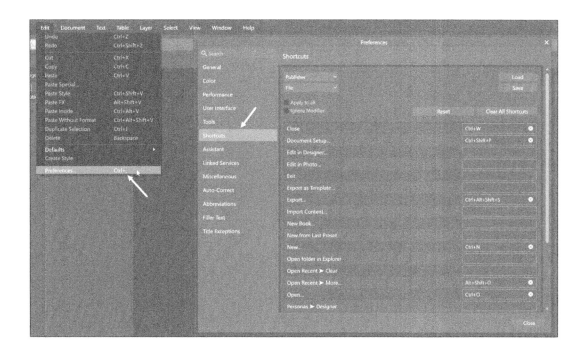

That will show all the available settings or tasks that can be assigned a shortcut. It will also display any shortcut that's already assigned to that setting or task.

You can modify an existing shortcut, although be careful since then your system won't work the way anyone else's does if you do that.

For the one I mentioned above, I used the second dropdown menu up top to choose Layer, and then scrolled down to find New Adjustment →Brightness/ Contrast. I then clicked into the field for that option and typed my shortcut. (I use Ctrl + ~ for that one.)

Click Close when done.

CONCLUSION

Okay, so there you have it, the basics of formatting a print interior using Affinity Publisher 2.0. Part 1 covered a basic title with a simple accent image. Part 2 expanded on that and covered tables of contents, indexes, inserting images into your text, and creating a file that merges multiple books into one.

As I've mentioned elsewhere, this has worked for me for formatting about a hundred books, but I may not have the perfect approach. I am the perennial A-student who does things good enough but not perfect, so if you find a better way to do it or want to do something differently than I showed you here, go for it.

My goal with these books was to short-cut the learning curve for you so that you didn't have to do the same watch videos, experiment, try, try again that I've had to do to learn this program.

Hopefully this helped. If you get stuck, reach out, I'm happy to see if I can find an answer for you.

Also, Affinity has very good help resources, so don't be afraid to do a quick internet search for Affinity Publisher and whatever you're trying to learn. From what I've seen their user forums also tend to be pretty cordial so if you ask a question there someone likely isn't going to jump all over you for not being perfect. (Unlike some other tech forums out there.)

Good luck with it. Don't do it if you hate it. For most books most readers are going to be just fine with a Vellum-formatted or similar book. But have fun with it if you do enjoy it.

The beauty of self-publishing, at least if you're using print on demand, is that you can change things if you want. Try something. Publish it. Decide you don't like it. Change it. Easy peasy.

Okay. Enjoy. And reach out if you get stuck.

APPENDIX A: QUICK TAKES

AUTHOR NAME

FIELD EDIT
Fields panel. Click on field next to Author. Type author name. Enter.

INSERT
Artistic Text Tool. Click on location in document where field should be inserted. Go to Fields panel. Double-click on Author.

BOOK TITLE

FIELD EDIT
Fields panel. Click on field next to Title. Type book title. Enter.

INSERT
Artistic Text Tool. Click on location in document where field should be inserted. Go to Fields panel. Double-click on Title.

CHAPTER TITLE

INSERT AS HEADER
Click on location in document. Go to top menu. Text→Insert Fields→ Section Name. Assign the chapter title to the section.

COLUMNS

BALANCE TEXT
Click on the text frame. Go to the Columns section of the Text Frame panel and click the "Balance Text Columns" box.

CHANGE NUMBER
Move Tool. Click on text frame. Go to dynamic menu up top and change value for Columns. Or use Columns section of the Text Frame panel.

DIVIDING LINE
Click on the text frame. Open the Text Frame panel and go to the Column Rules section and change the Stroke settings. Top and Bottom values will

determine whether the line fills the entire space. Start and End dropdowns can be used to put a shape at the end of the divider line, like an arrow.

FORMAT

Click on the text frame. Open the Text Frame panel and go to the Columns section.

GAP BETWEEN

Click on text frame. Go to dynamic menu up top and change the number in the field to the right of the number of columns setting. Or open the Text Frame panel and go to the Columns section and adjust the value for the gutter.

DOCUMENT PRESET

CREATE

Use the New dialogue box to specify all document settings. When done, click on the icon with a plus sign next to the name for the document. In the Create Preset dialogue box type a name for the document preset, choose an icon, and choose a Category.

DELETE

Right-click on document preset in the New dialogue box and choose Delete Preset.

MOVE DOCUMENT PRESET TO NEW CATEGORY

In the New dialogue box, left-click on the document preset in the document preset listing, and drag to the new category.

NEW CATEGORY

In the New dialogue box, at the bottom of the listing of document presets, click on the icon for Create Category. Type the category name in the New Category dialogue box. OK.

RENAME

Right-click on document preset in the New dialogue box and choose Rename Preset. Type new name into Rename Preset dialogue box. OK.

EXPORT

PDF

To export a PDF of your document, go to File→Export, and choose the PDF option. For review purposes, All Spreads is better because it will keep facing pages together in the PDF. For KDP and IngramSpark upload, use All Pages.

IMAGE

ADJUSTMENTS

To adjust an image, click on the image layer, go to Layer→New Adjustment and choose the type of image adjustment you need. You can also use the Adjustments option at the bottom of the Layers panel.

CENTER

Left-click and drag the image until you see the green center line. For a standard book, be sure to drag from the outer edge of the page because there will be two center lines, one for the entire page and one for the text frame. Lines will only be visible when Snapping is turned on.

For a pinned image, use the Pinning panel.

DPI

The image DPI will increase as your image size decreases. For print, images should have a minimum DPI of 300. You can change the minimum DPI for the document by going to File→Document Setup→Document and changing the DPI setting there.

FLOAT

To float an image, open the Pinning panel and click on the Float tab.

IMPORT PREFERENCES WITH PICTURE FRAME

When importing an image into a picture frame, you can set how the image imports using the Preferences option in the dynamic menu after you click on the picture frame.

INLINE

To make an image an inline image, open the Pinning panel and click on the Inline tab.

INSERT

Place Image Tool. Select image to insert. Open. Image may automatically insert. If not, click and drag in workspace until desired size.

INSERT IN PICTURE FRAME

Click on picture frame layer. Place Image Tool. Select image to insert. Open. Your import preferences will determine if the image comes in at the document DPI or at a size that best fits the picture frame.

MOVE

Move Tool. Click on image layer or directly on image if not in a picture frame. Click on image, hold left-click and drag to desired location. Use Snapping to align along edges or center.

MOVE PIN

For a pinned image, you can left-click and drag on the pin to move what text the image is pinned to.

PIN TO TEXT

If you click into your text before inserting an image, the image will be pinned to your text when it inserts. If an image is not pinned to text, you can use the Pinning panel or the pin option in the dynamic menu up top to pin the image to your text after the fact.

QUALITY

For print files, use a DPI of at least 300 for grayscale images and 600 for black and white line drawings. Go to File→Document Setup to specify your document DPI. Set it slightly above the desired DPI if importing images.

REPLACE

Document top menu. Window→Resource Manager. Select image. Replace. Select new image. Open. Close resource manager.

Or. Move Tool selected, click on image, use Replace Image option in dynamic menu. Choose new image. Open

RESIZE

Move Tool. Click on image layer or directly on image if not in a picture frame.

Option A: Transform panel. Lock Aspect Ratio. Change height or width value.

Option B: Click on blue circle in corner and drag at an angle to resize proportionately. Or click on blue circle along any edge to change height or width only. This will skew most images.

UNPIN

Layers panel. Click on image layer. Open Pinning panel. Click on Unpin.

WRAP

To have text jump or wrap around an inserted image, click on the image and then use the Show Text Wrap Settings in the top menu to choose the Wrap Style.

INDEX

INSERT

Click into document where you want to place the index. Go to the Index panel. Click on the Insert Index option.

Or click into the document, go to the top menu, Text→Index→Insert Index.

MANUAL EDITS

Once inserted, an index can be manually edited but those edits will be overwritten if the index is ever updated.

TEXT STYLE

The index entries use text styles so text can be edited and then the text style updated to apply that change to all entries.

UPDATE

Go to the top menu and then Text→Index→Update Index.

Or use the Index panel and choose the Update option at the top. If the index does not update, delete the existing text of the index, and insert a new index instead.

INDEX MARKERS AND TOPICS

CROSS-REFERENCE

Right-click on the topic you want to cross-reference from and choose Add Cross Reference. In the Add Cross-Reference dialogue box select the topic you want to reference to in the dropdown menu.

INSERT

Select the text you want to use as your index text or click into the text where you want the marker. Either go to the Index panel and click on the Insert Marker option at the top or go to the top menu, Text→Index→Insert Index Mark.

MOVE ENTRY LEVEL

Go to the Index panel and left-click on the topic name you want to move. Drag it to the topic you want to place it under.

Or right-click on the topic name choose to Edit Topic and change the Parent Topic information to either add or remove a parent level.

NAME (ASSIGN)

In the Insert Index Mark dialogue box type the name into the Topic Name field.

NAME (EDIT)

Click once on the name. Click again to select the text. Type in your new name.

Or right-click, Edit Topic, and change the value in the Topic Name field.

PARENT TOPIC (ASSIGN)

Open the Insert Index Mark dialogue box or the Edit Index Mark dialogue box and choose the parent topic you want from the Parent Topic dropdown menu.

PARENT TOPIC (REMOVE PAGE NUMBERING)

To remove any underlying citations from the Parent Topic in the Index panel either move them to a subtopic or delete them by clicking on each entry and using the trash can icon at the top of the panel.

MASTER PAGE

ADD NEW

Pages panel. Master Pages section. Right-click on existing master page.

Option A: Choose Insert Master. Click OK to create a new master page that has the basic properties of the existing master page.

Option B: Choose Duplicate to create an exact duplicate of the existing master page.

MOVE

Pages panel. Master Pages section. Left-click on master page and drag. Blue line along edge will show where master page will move to. Release left-click when positioned where wanted.

RENAME

Pages panel. Master pages section. Click on master page thumbnail. Click on name of master page. Type in new name. Enter.

MERGE DOCUMENTS

ADD DOCUMENT

Go to the page of the existing document in the Pages panel where you want to add the document, right-click, and choose Add Pages From File from the dropdown. Navigate to and select the document to import. In the Add Pages dialogue box choose All Pages, After, Pages, and verify that it shows the page number for that page. OK.

PRE-IMPORT SET-UP

If your documents are set to have a right-hand page start, be sure that the document you're importing into has only one page on the left-hand side at the end in order to maintain pages on the correct side of the page.

PAGE NUMBER

CHANGE NUMBERING STYLE

Pages panel. Pages section. Right-click on page and choose Edit Section. Click on section name that contains the pages where you want to change the numbering style if not already visible. Choose the new style from the Number Style dropdown menu. Close.

INSERT

Master page. Artistic Text Tool. Click where you want page number placed. Go to top menu, Text→Insert→Fields→Page Number.

RESTART AT 1

Pages panel. Pages section. Right-click on page where you want to restart at 1. Start New Section. (Or Edit Section if one has already been started.) Click button for Restart Page Numbering At. Enter 1. Change numbering style if needed. Close.

PAGES

ADD PAGES

Pages panel. Pages section. Right-click on an existing page or page spread. Add Pages. Choose the number of pages to add, whether to insert before or after that location, and choose the master page to use for the inserted pages. OK.

APPLY MASTER PAGE

Pages panel. Pages section. Right-click on the pages where you want to apply the master page. (Be sure that both pages are selected in a two-page spread.) Apply Master. Choose desired master page from dropdown menu. OK.

DELETE PAGES

Pages panel. Pages section. Select pages or page spreads that you want to delete. Right-click. Delete X Pages.

SELECT

If you only want to edit one page in a two-page spread, be sure to click on just that side of the page spread. Only that one page should be surrounded by a blue border.

If there is more than page spread that you want to select, click on the first page or page spread at one end of the page range, hold down the shift key and click on the last page or page spread at the other end of the page range.

PANEL

CLOSE
To close a panel either go to the Window menu and click on the panel name or left-click and drag the panel until it is standalone in your workspace and then click on the X in the top right corner.

MOVE OR ANCHOR
Left-click on panel tab and drag to desired location. To anchor, either drag until you see a blue box appear and then release or drag to where other panels are already anchored and add to those tabs.

OPEN
To open a panel go to the Window menu and click on the panel name. Some panels are listed in secondary dropdown menus.

PICTURE FRAME

BORDER
Click on the Picture Frame. Go to the dynamic menu up top and use the Stroke option to add a color to create a border or click on the line next to it to change the border width.

INSERT
Picture Frame Rectangle Tool. Click and drag to create frame on canvas.

JUMP
To have text jump an inserted picture frame, click on the Picture Frame and then use the Show Text Wrap Settings in the top menu and choose Jump for the Wrap Style.

RESIZE TO IMAGE
Click on Picture Frame and in dynamic menu choose the Size Frame to Content option.

WRAP TEXT AROUND

To have text wrap around an inserted picture frame, click on the Picture Frame and then use the Show Text Wrap Settings in the top menu and choose Square or Tight for the Wrap Style.

RECOVER FILE

RECOVER FILE

If Affinity ever crashes and closes while you were working on a file, reopen the program and try to reopen the file. Affinity should tell you that there is a recovery version of the file available. Choose to open the recovery version and then check for the last edits you made to determine if any of your work was lost and needs to be redone.

SECTION

ASSIGN NAME

Pages panel. Pages section. Right-click on the page at the start of the section and either Edit Section or Start New Section. In Section Manager type name into Section Name field. Close.

CHANGE START PAGE

Pages panel. Pages section. Right-click and Edit Section. In Section Manager, change the "Start On Page".

CONTINUE PAGE NUMBERING

Pages panel. Pages section. Right-click and Edit Section to open Section Manager. Click on the section that needs to continue page numbering and check the box to continue page numbering.

CREATE

Pages panel. Pages section. Right-click on the page that you want to have start the new section, Start New Section. In Section Manager, assign name if desired and verify page numbering format and whether it should restart or continue.

EDIT

Pages panel. Pages section. Right-click and Edit Section.

DELETE

Pages panel. Pages section. Right-click and Edit Section. In Section Manager, click on the section you want to delete and use the small trash can icon to delete it.

INSERT NAME

Click on location in header where field should be inserted. Go to top menu, Text →Insert→Fields→Section Name.

RESTART PAGE NUMBERING

Pages panel. Pages section. Right-click and Edit Section. For the section that needs to restart page numbering, check the box to "restart page numbering at", verify the page number, generally 1, and the number style.

SNAPPING

ENABLE

Go to the horseshoe shaped magnet image in the top center. Click on the dropdown arrow. Check the box next to Enable Snapping.

USE

To use snapping, as you move an object around in your workspace Affinity will show either green or red lines on the workspace when the object is aligned with the edges or center of other objects on the page.

STUDIO PRESET

ADD NEW

Arrange panels as desired. Go to top menu. Window→Studio→Add Preset. Type name. OK.

APPLY

Top menu. Window→Studio. Select desired preset. Or use Ctrl + Shift + [Number] preset for that studio.

DELETE

Window→Studio→Manage Studio Presets. Select preset name. Delete. Close.

RENAME
Window→Studio→Manage Studio Presets. Select preset name. Rename. Type in new name. OK.

SAVE CHANGES
Make desired changes to panel preset arrangement. Window→Studio→Add Preset. Type in exact same name as before. OK. Agree to overwrite old preset.

TABLE OF CONTENTS

ENTRIES (SELECT)
Assign one or more unique text styles to each text entry in the document that you want included in the table of contents. Go to the Table of Contents panel and under Style Name, check the check box for each text style you want to include.

ENTRIES (MANUAL UPDATE)
You can manually update any text in the table of contents, but it is better to update the text in the document and then refresh your table of contents.

ENTRIES (WHEN NO TEXT AVAILABLE FOR SELECTION)
If you ever have a situation where you need a table of contents entry but there is no visible text to use for it, you can create a text frame on that page, place that text you need into the frame, assign a text style to it that you are using in the table of contents, and then hide the frame.

FOR SECTION
To insert a table of contents that covers only a section of a book, insert the table of contents like normal but be sure to check the box for "Stop at Next TOC" and to use different text styles than the ones used in the overarching table of contents.

INSERT
Click into the document where you want your table of contents inserted.

Option A: Go to the Table of Contents panel, click on the Insert option on the left at the top.

Option B: Top menu, Text→Table of Contents→Insert Table of Contents.

OVERARCHING

For a table of contents that covers the entire document when other tables of contents exist in the document, be sure to use specific text styles for just that table of contents and to NOT check the "Stop at Next TOC" option.

PAGE NUMBERS

To include page numbers in your table of contents entries, right-click on the preferences dropdown for that text style and check the box for "Include Page Number." To remove page numbers, uncheck it.

SEPARATORS BETWEEN TEXT AND PAGE NUMBER

Go to the Separator section of the Table of Contents panel. Use the dropdown menu to select your desired separator or type into the field.

For a dotted line or solid line, right-click on the text style in the Text Styles panel, and choose to edit it. Go to the Tab Stops section and choose the desired Tab Stop Leader Character option.

UPDATE

Go to the Table of Contents panel and click on the Update option at the top. If you have multiple tables of contents in your document, be sure the TOC dropdown shows the table of contents you want to update or choose to update all.

Or go to Text→Table of Contents→Update Table of Contents.

Or click on Fix in the Preflight panel when it says one or more table of contents need updated.

TEXT

ADD SPACE BETWEEN LINES

Artistic Text Tool. Select paragraph of text. Paragraph panel. Spacing section. Leading dropdown. Choose desired option. Or for multiple lines of the same style, click on Space Between Same Styles and set a value.

ADD SPECIAL SYMBOLS OR CHARACTERS

Artistic Text Tool. Click into workspace where desired. Go to the Glyph Browser panel. (Window→Text→Glyph Browser if not open.) Find desired symbol or character. Double-click on symbol or character to insert.

ALIGNMENT

Artistic Text Tool. Click on the paragraph or select the paragraphs. Dynamic menu choices above workspace. Four images with lines. Align Left, Align Center, Align Right, or dropdown menu for Justify Left, Justify Center, Justify Right, Justify All, Align Towards Spine, Align Away From Spine. Or, to the right of that, dropdown menu for Top Align, Center Vertically, Bottom Align, Justify Vertically.

The horizontal alignment options are also available at the top of the Paragraph panel.

ALL CAPS OR SMALL CAPS

Artistic Text Tool. Select the text to be formatted. Go to Character panel. Typography section. Click on the two capital Ts to apply all caps. Click on the capital T with a smaller capital T to apply small caps. Check your text entries for issues with using a capital letter or lower case letter when working with small caps because the two do look different in small caps.

BOLD

Artistic Text Tool. Select text. Font Style dropdown menu, Ctrl + B, or click on B in top menu.

Or go to Character panel and choose the Strong option from the Character Style dropdown menu at the top or use the Font Style dropdown menu.

Only works if there is a bold version of the font available.

FONT

Artistic Text Tool. Select text. Top menu, left-hand side. Font Family dropdown. Choose font.

Or select text and go to Character panel and use the Font Family dropdown at top.

HYPHENATION

Artistic Text Tool. Select text. Paragraph panel. Hyphenation section. Click on box next to Use Auto-Hyphenation. Change values as needed.

INDENT PARAGRAPH

Artistic Text Tool. Select paragraph. Paragraph panel. Spacing section. Second option on left-hand side. (First Line Indent). Add value.

ITALICS

Artistic Text Tool. Select text. Font Style dropdown menu, Ctrl + I, or click on I in top menu.

Or go to Character panel and choose the Emphasis option from the Character Style dropdown menu at the top or use the Font Style dropdown.

Only works if there is an italic version of the font available.

JUMP IMAGE

Move Tool. Select image. Click on Show Text Wrap Settings option in top menu. In Text Wrap dialogue box choose Jump as desired Wrap Style.

KEEP TOGETHER

Artistic Text Tool. Select second paragraph that you want to keep together. Go to the Paragraph panel. Flow Options section. Check box for Keep With Previous Paragraph.

LINE SPACING (LEADING)

Artistic Text Tool. Select paragraph. Paragraph panel. Spacing section. Change value in Leading dropdown. Default is usually a good place to start.

MOVE TO NEXT PAGE

Click right after the text that's before the text you want to move to the next page. Go to Text→Insert→Break→Frame Break to move the text to the next frame or →Page Break to move to next page.

ORPHANS REMOVE AUTOMATICALLY

Paragraph panel. Flow Options. Check box for Prevent Orphaned First Lines.

SIZE

Artistic Text Tool. Select text. Top menu, left-hand side. Font Size dropdown. Choose size or type in size.

Or select text and go to Character panel and use the Font Size dropdown at top.

SMALL CAPS

See *All Caps or Small Caps*.

TRACKING

Artistic Text Tool. Select text. Character panel. Positioning and Transform section. Second option in the left-hand column, Tracking. Click arrow for dropdown menu. Choose desired change.

UNDERLINE

Artistic Text Tool. Select text. Ctrl + U or click on the underlined U in top menu.

Or go to Character panel and choose one of the underlined U options from the Decorations section.

WEIGHT

Artistic Text Tool. Select text. Top menu, left-hand side. Font Style dropdown. Choose from available weights for that font.

Or select text and go to Character panel Font Style dropdown at top.

WIDOWS REMOVE AUTOMATICALLY

Paragraph panel. Flow Options. Check box for Prevent Widowed Last Lines.

WRAP AROUND IMAGE

Move Tool. Select image. Click on Show Text Wrap Settings option in top menu. In Text Wrap dialogue box choose Wrap Style.

TEXT FLOW

AUTO FLOW

Pages panel. Pages section. Double-click on last page spread in section. Go to right-hand edge of last text frame in workspace. Click on red circle to see red arrow. Hold down shift key and click on red arrow. Affinity will flow the text to as many page spreads as needed using the same master page spread format as the last one.

FROM ONE TEXT FRAME TO ANOTHER (ADD)

Click on blue arrow along the edge of the first text frame. Click on second text frame.

FROM ONE TEXT FRAME TO ANOTHER (REMOVE)

Click on the blue arrow along the edge of the first text frame. Click back onto the first text frame. If arrow is not visible, click on that text frame first.

TEXT FRAME

CHANGE SIZE

Frame Text Tool or Move Tool. Click on text frame or layer for text frame in Layers panel. Use Transform panel to input specific values or use blue circles around perimeter and left-click and drag.

ALIGN OR POSITION

Frame Text Tool or Move Tool. Left-click on text frame and hold as you drag. Look for red and green alignment lines to center or align to other elements in workspace. (Turn on Snapping if there are no red or green lines.)

INSERT

Frame Text Tool. Click and drag in workspace.

TEXT STYLE

APPLY

Artistic Text Tool. Select text. Use dropdown menu at top to apply style. Or go to Text Styles panel and click on desired style. Or use shortcut if one is associated with the style.

BASED ON OTHER STYLE

To base a text style off of another style, first apply the existing text style. Next, make any edits to create the new style. Finally, save as new style.

IMPORTED

If you use the import text style option or are merging two files and it appears, you can choose which text styles to import using the checkbox on the far left. If this is for an import with overlapping text style names click on the Rename To option to bring in the text style but with a new name, click on OK to bring it in with the same name, or choose which of the two styles to keep if there is a conflict identified.

KEYBOARD SHORTCUT

For a new style, add a keyboard shortcut in the Style section of the Create Paragraph Style dialogue box where it says Keyboard Shortcut. (Don't type the description, just use the shortcut when you're clicked into the box.) For an existing style, go to the Text Styles panel, right-click on the style name, Edit [Style Name], and then in the Style section of the Edit Text Style dialogue box, add the keyboard shortcut.

NEW

Artistic Text Tool. Select text. Format text. Style dropdown in top menu. New Style. Give style a name and keyboard shortcut if desired. OK.

UPDATE OR CHANGE

Artistic Text Tool. Select text with style to be updated. Make edits. Click on Update Paragraph Style option to the right of the style dropdown menu in the top menu area.

Or, go to Text Styles panel, right-click on text style name, Edit [Style Name], make edits in Edit Text Style dialogue box, OK.

APPENDIX B: CREATE A BOOK
FROM AN EXISTING FILE

1. Delete out any old text from the main body of the existing file and delete all pages except the front matter, first chapter start page, and the first Text and Text page.

2. If you want to use different fonts in your document than are used in the existing file, change the fonts for the relevant text styles. If your document is set up with primary and secondary text styles then you only need to change the primary text style for each font.

3. Replace the image(s) in the document or delete the images from the master pages, if needed.

4. After you've replaced any image, make sure it is still positioned properly on each master page.

5. Edit the text on the Title page to reflect the correct book title.

6. Edit the text on the Also By page to reflect the correct series name(s) and title name(s).

7. Edit the text on the Copyright page to show the copyright year, copyright name, and ISBN for the title.

8. Go to the Fields panel and edit the Author and Title fields to show the correct author name and book title.

9. Paste in the main body text of your document.

10. If your text imported with an assigned style or styles, you can use find and replace to change the assigned styles to the ones you need. Otherwise, apply the main body text style for now.

11. Flow your text by Shift + clicking on the red arrow on the right-hand edge of the right-hand text box of the last page which should be a Text and Text page.

12. Assign chapter header and paragraph text styles to the first page of the main body of the book. Double-check that the document looks good. That all images are placed properly, chapter starts are where you want them, paragraphs are formatted as desired, etc. If not, fix those issues in your master pages or text styles before proceeding.

13. Walk through your main body text and assign chapter header, first paragraph, and section break formatting to the text as needed. Also change the master page assigned for each spread when needed. And fix any widows, orphans, one-line chapter ends, etc.

14. Italicize or bold text that was overwritten when the text styles were applied.

15. At the end of the document you may need to either reflow the text again to cover all of your text and/or there may be extra pages that weren't used that need to be deleted.

16. Add your back matter. At a minimum this should include an About the Author page.

17. Export to PDF.

18. Review the PDF file and verify that all pages exported and look as expected. Specifically check headers, footers, paragraph formatting, master page assignment, chapter header and section break formatting, front matter, and back matter. Also check for single-line chapter endings, widows, orphans, short words at the end of paragraphs, and too much white space in justified paragraphs.

19. For any issues, fix them in the Affinity file and then re-export and re-review. Repeat as needed.

20. When final, Export to PDF (PDF X-1a:2003 should work for most purposes) being sure to change the Area selection to All Pages from All Spreads. The PDF should be ready to upload for printing.

INDEX

ABOUT THE AUTHOR

M.L. Humphrey is a self-published author with both fiction and non-fiction titles published under a variety of pen names.

You can reach her at:

mlhumphreywriter@gmail.com

or at

www.mlhumphrey.com

Made in the USA
Middletown, DE
22 September 2024